A Blueprint Monograph

Queensberry Hun

Susannah Walker

Creativity and industry

Published by Fourth Estate
and Wordsearch Ltd

*Previous page:
The Queensberry Hunt
Partnership: John Horler,
David Queensberry, Martin
Hunt and Robin Levien*

First Published in
Great Britain in 1992 by
Fourth Estate Ltd,
289 Westbourne Grove,
London W11 2QA in
conjunction with *Blueprint*
magazine, 26 Cramer
Street, London W1M 3HE

A catalogue record for this
book is available from the
British Library.

ISBN 1 857 020 111

Design: Stephen Coates
Series Editor:
Arthur Valenzuela
Colour reproduction:
Positive Colour Limited,
Malden, Essex, UK
Printed and bound
in Portugal

Photographic credits
Phil Sayer: front cover, 2-3,
8, 22, 40, 52, 66-87, 88.

Acknowledgements
With thanks to all the
people who helped with
the research for the book,
especially Terence Conran,
Colin Rawson, Sir Arthur
Bryan, Pat Freeman,
Frank Ridge, Mike Watson,
Roger Cooper, John
Laughton, Oliver Watson,
Jennifer Opie, Paul
Greenhalgh, and Tanya
Rebuck at the V&A, and
of course everyone at
Queensberry Hunt.

Susannah Walker is
the guest curator of
the Victoria and Albert
Museum's exhibition on
the work of Queensberry
Hunt mounted in 1992.

Blueprint Monographs
*Ron Arad:
Restless Furniture*
Deyan Sudjic
*Nigel Coates:
The City in Motion*
Rick Poynor
*Rei Kawakubo and
Comme des Garçons*
Deyan Sudjic
Eva Jiricna: Design in Exile
Martin Pawley
*King and Miranda:
The Poetry of the Machine*
Hugh Aldersey-Williams
*Javier Mariscal:
Designing the New Spain*
Emma Dent-Coad
*Rodney Kinsman:
The Logical Art of Furniture*
Jose Manser
*Stansted:
Norman Foster and the
Architecture of Flight*
Kenneth Powell
Rick Mather
Hugh Pearman

Contents

A new kind of partnership

Queensberry Hunt, the partnership started by David Queensberry and Martin Hunt in 1966, has managed to straddle what many believe to be the unbridgeable chasm between design and commercial success. Not only do their designs sell consistently, they have also won numerous awards and can be found in permanent collections such as the Victoria and Albert Museum. They have specialised in ceramics and tableware, where their work has been particularly influential, but have also received critical acclaim for designs in fields as diverse as bathroom sanitary ware and telephones.

What is equally remarkable is the fact that the partnership, now expanded to four members, has been in existence for more than twenty-five years. It is rare for a coalition of designers to maintain this degree of stability; to be still working together amicably and producing good work over such a period of time is an even more unusual achievement. Part of the reason for this consistency undoubtedly stems from their personalities, and from the early days David Queensberry and Martin Hunt have formed a very complementary pairing. Terence Conran, who has known and worked with David Queensberry for over thirty years, attributes some of Queensberry Hunt's success to this compatibility: "I actually think of Martin as more of a designer and David more of a business man. Martin is a bit unwordly as the commercial world goes, and David is really devoted to seeing the shelves stacked with china. I think that it is a very good combination."

The nature of the Queensberry Hunt partnership has of course evolved somewhat from the time when, based initially at the Royal College of Art, it consisted of only David Queensberry and Martin Hunt, taking on private commissions while still teaching. They have since recruited two more partners, Robin Levien and John Horler, moved out of the college, and expanded until the partnership at one point employed fourteen people. For David Queensberry, working with younger designers has always been a deliberate policy. He is certain that only by bringing in new people can the partnership hope to produce fresh work: "Design is a job for young people. Most creative work is done by the under-forties, not by people my age. I believe that more young people should be encouraged to have their say in design, be given opportunities and be well rewarded financially." However, even with the introduction of new partners and more employees, Queensberry Hunt has still managed to maintain a co-operative and intimate way of working, something which everyone involved in the partnership wants to preserve for the foreseeable future. They certainly have no intention of growing into a large design corporation. Robin Levien emphasises: "It is a lifestyle issue really. Are you keeping this huge monster going or are you having a fairly relaxed time, enjoying what you are doing and making a good enough living out of it? In that sense, I envisage the size of Queensberry Hunt staying pretty much as it is."

In the broader picture, the history of Queensberry Hunt over the last twenty five years has mirrored the emergence of a recognisable design industry in Britain in the same period of time. Queensberry Hunt was one of the first wave of design consultancies to be formed in the fifties and sixties, however, as design became a recognised profession in the expanding market of the seventies and eighties, Queensberry Hunt have become just one of many product design consultancies. The way in which the nature of their work has evolved over time might also be seen to reflect broader changes in the British design industry as a whole. From, at first, working for several British firms who were committed to making good contemporary design, they have increasingly found themselves working for companies abroad, initially in Europe and more recently in the Far East.

Something which distinguishes Queensberry Hunt from many other consultancies is the fact that so many of their designs sell in large numbers. Trend, which was designed for the German manufacturers Thomas, has become the best-selling contemporary tableware in Europe over the last ten years. One of Queensberry Hunt's primary aims is to produce designs that will be a commercial success. An indication of how central this is to their philosophy is the fact that they prefer to work on a royalty basis, which means that they have a direct financial incentive to produce designs which will be successful in the market. However, this does not mean that they design in an undiscriminatingly commercial manner – the partnership also has a genuine passion for good design. They have deliberately sought to prove that good design and mass market appeal are not irreconcilable concepts, and at least part of their success is due to the fact that they only design products which they believe in. Martin Hunt explains: "From the start we have always tried to design the sort of things that we like ourselves. That is a privilege of being freelance – you can hold on to your principles and wave a small flag. But it is not just an matter of principles, we do best that which excites us."

This desire to produce good design for everyday life is in some respects part of a certain inherent Englishness in their approach to design. It derives from attitudes prevalent in the fifties which were part of the formative experiences of David Queensberry at least. Design from this period has been defined as concerned with everyday ordinary things, unpretentious and representative of good craftsmanship. This would provide a very apt description of the work of Queensberry Hunt, in particular its emphasis on the craft aspect. They have fed this tradition into their work, and their methods are distinguished by a craft-like concern for detail, for materials and the skill of their modelmaking, so that a design for mass production can come out of a very craft-like process of hands-on design and discovery. The result of these methods are designs which are not dramatic designer statements, but instead have a simple but effective form, and are very easy to use and live with.

It is an unusual approach, and although it is not a policy which in general elicits headlines from design journalists, it is one which has brought them a lasting reputation in their fields and which has made them one of the most consistently successful of British product design consultancies.

Chapter One

The studio and the factory

David Queensberry's second design for Midwinter from 1966, known as MQ2

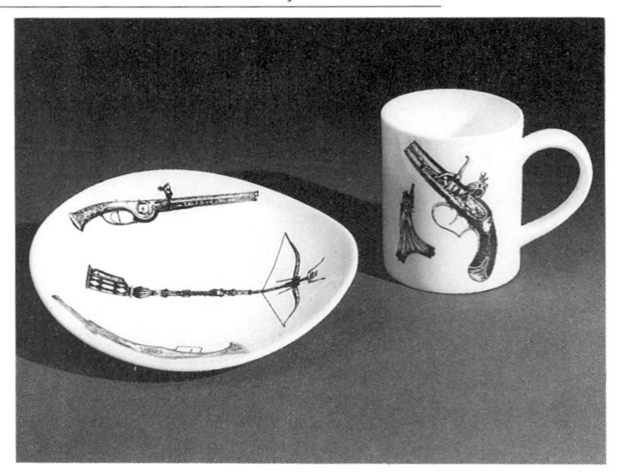

Left and below: David Queensberry's designs for Crown Staffordshire China brought contemporary design into bone china. The graphics on these pieces were commissioned by David Queensberry from Tom Taylor

Despite the role that the Royal College of Art would play in the later history of Queensberry Hunt, David Queensberry's first encounter with the place could not really be said to be auspicious. After a relatively undistinguished school career at Eton, his interest had only really been stimulated by the pottery run by an eccentric art master. After completing his National Service, David Queensberry had been recommended to the Royal College in 1950 by this same art teacher, who knew the Rector, Robin Darwin. The then Head of Ceramics, Professor Baker, was less than pleased at having a pupil foisted on him in this manner, not least because of his firm belief that the greatest skill that a ceramic designer required was the ability to produce detailed flower drawings for decoration, a field in which David Queensberry singularly failed to excel. Moreover, Queensberry's real interests were in three-dimensional design and how things were made – something that he feels is true of almost all ceramic designers. Queensberry was unimpressed with the course of study, and so it was perhaps not surprising then that he parted company with Baker and the Royal College after only one term.

Even after Queensberry had spent some time on Chelsea's Fine Art course in an attempt to improve his flower-drawing skills, Professor Baker was still reluctant to

The Crown Staffordshire range also included these contemporary vases, inspired by the radio masts and aerials adjacent to the A5 at Rugby

readmit him, so Queensberry decided instead to spend two years on the pottery course at the Central School of Art. Here at least the emphasis was on three-dimensional design, although the ethos was very much that of the arts and crafts movement, and the course was geared to the needs of studio potters rather than industrial production. All in all, the course was, in David Queensberry's opinion, "abysmally ignorant about how something as simple as a dinner plate was made, fired and decorated."

At various points, Queensberry did consider becoming a studio potter, but because he doubted whether he would ever become truly outstanding, he decided instead to pursue his fascination with industry. "I wasn't a good enough artist, and anyway, I didn't want to be arty-crafty. Why spend your life making by hand what a machine can do so much better?" In the end it seemed to Queensberry that the only way to learn about the industrial manufacture of pottery would be to go up to somewhere like Stoke on Trent, where the process actually took place. Stoke was, as it still is, the centre of an extensive tableware industry which at that time comprised hundreds of small family firms producing all types of ware for both domestic and export markets. The industry was the despair of reforming bodies such as the Council of Industrial Design because modern design had made very little impact on the industry – indeed, it was barely an issue. Despite the success of modern designers such as Clarice Cliff and Susie Cooper in the thirties, most firms still made a more than adequate living from traditional patterns and shapes unaltered for a century. There seemed very little reason to change. Gradually, in the mid-fifties and early sixties a few firms had achieved a modest success selling modern, fashionable designs, but the backbone of the industry still remained the traditional styles.

Queensberry moved up to Stoke in the mid-fifties, making use of his only contact there to get a job as a very junior laboratory assistant, while at the same time taking day-release courses at the technical college. This rather humble approach gave David Queensberry an unusual level of inside knowledge, for a designer, about the technology and techniques of pottery. "One thing I discovered very quickly was that, from a technical and commercial point of view, all I had learned at art college was totally unrelated to industry." This grounding within the industry itself is something which he sees as having been crucial to the success of Queensberry Hunt. His wide range of technical experience means that, as Queensberry puts it: "People in the industry can't technically bullshit me," and he is always

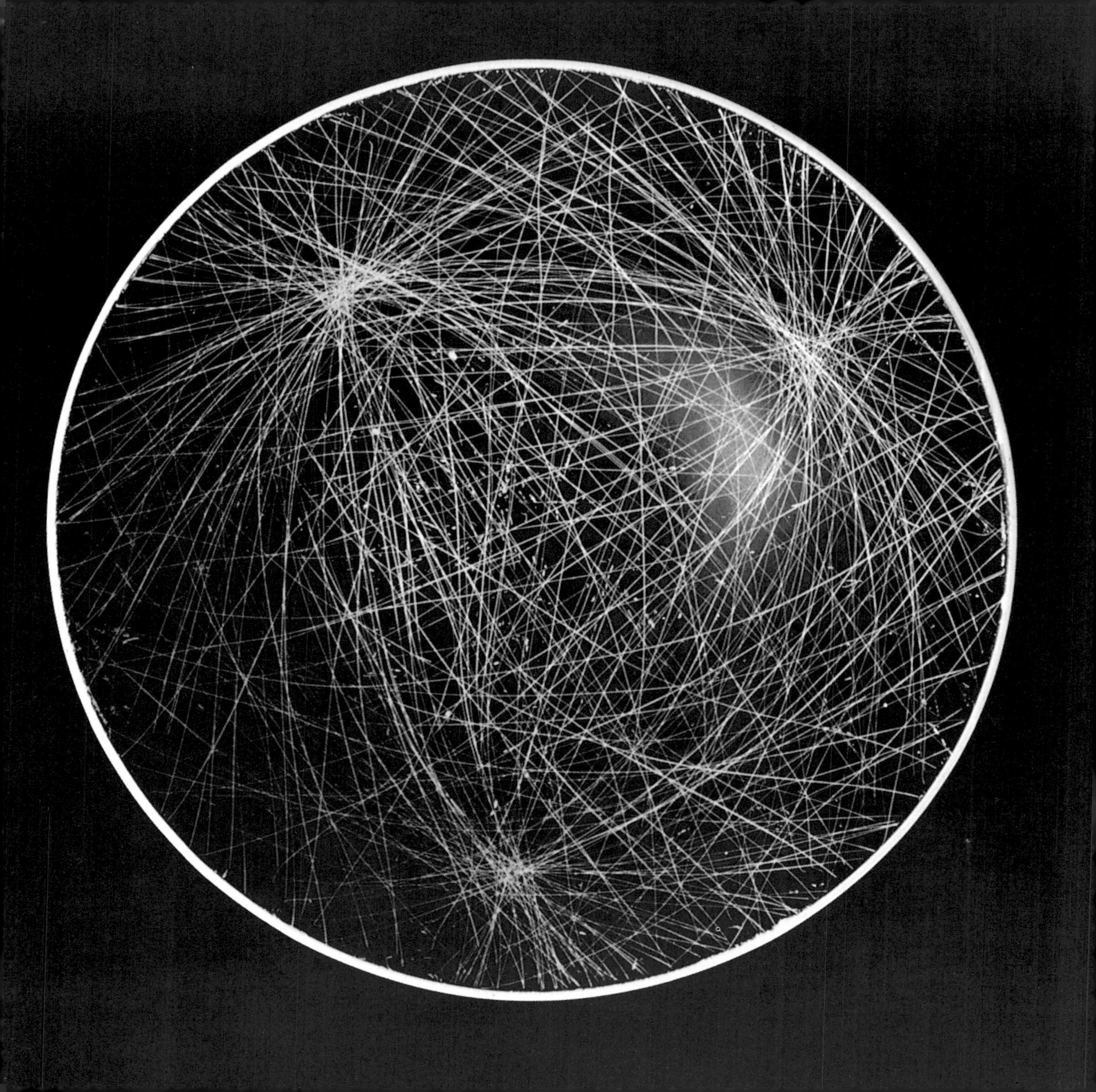

Left and opposite: The designs on these Crown Staffordshire bowls are produced by sgraffito, where a layer of on-glaze colour is scratched through to reveal the white china beneath

able to argue with a manufacturer who tells him that a design cannot be produced.

Moreover, working in Stoke also yielded further contacts with manufacturers who were prepared to make products that Queensberry had designed. The first big opportunity in this direction came from Sam Green, the director of Crown Staffordshire China, and in 1955 the firm produced a range of Queensberry's designs for "contemporary" bone china. The range was not a huge commercial success since, despite the sales of modern design in earthenware, purchasers of bone china still preferred to stick to more traditional and reassuring designs. However, the design did win acclaim from the Council of Industrial Design and finished second in their awards for "elegant design" in 1959. Queensberry had begun to make a name for himself as a designer of modern tableware.

Perhaps the most surprising result of this growing reputation was Queensberry's appointment as Professor of Ceramics at the Royal College of Art in 1959 at the age of just 29. Relations with Professor Baker did not seem to have improved when Queensberry attended an interview for the post, and he assumed that their former disagreements had ruined any chance of his being chosen. It transpired though that Robin Darwin, who was then running the college, was looking for a very different approach to the teaching of ceramic design and so Queensberry was taken on.

During Professor Baker's time, the college had run one of the few courses in the country to be devoted to the teaching of industrial ceramic techniques. However, the course had been defined by asking British manufacturers what kind of designers they required. Since firms replied that they needed students who could produce new but traditional-looking floral designs, this was what was taught. David Queensberry believed this to be a particularly narrow approach; "The RCA is to do with excellence and not what the unadventurous industry in Stoke on Trent thinks it needs at the moment." He felt that the college ought to be a centre of innovation, but what it was producing at the time was not even challenging the manufacturers in Stoke, merely emulating them. Instead, Queensberry believed that the course should be looking to places like Germany and Scandinavia, where the innovative work of the period was being made, and so after his appointment he set out to broaden the scope of the course, making contact with firms in Europe and taking students on visits there.

Under David Queensberry's leadership, the course at the Royal College also expanded over time from being one

David Queensberry's Fine shape for Midwinter, left and opposite, set the trends in tableware for the first half of the sixties. The gravy boat was particularly innovative in that its handle is directly derived from Lucy Rie's side-handled jugs of the same period

intended exclusively for students of industrial techniques to one which took on a considerable number of studio potters each year. Queensberry felt it had been ludicrous to exclude studio work from the college, and that there were positive advantages for people studying design to be mixing with people who are doing studio ceramics. He therefore employed as tutors Eduardo Paolozzi, a life-long friend, and Hans Coper, who was the leading studio ceramist living and working in Britain. Under Queensberry's tutelage, some of the foremost figures in the development of studio ceramics studied at the Royal College. The department did, however, continue to teach botanical illustration as a necessary skill for ceramic decoration if that was what students chose to study.

Queensberry still continued with his own design work even while teaching at the Royal College. This had started in the mid-fifties, when a series of commissions designing tableware for new and fashionable restaurants had brought him into contact with Terence Conran, who was designing the interiors. Despite the fact that their relationship began when Terence Conran pinched David Queensberry's girlfriend (she later became Shirley Conran), the pair managed to remain friends and business associates over the years. And at the end of the decade, it was Conran who introduced Queensberry to Roy Midwinter, a manufacturer who was to become a vital contact and friend over the years. Midwinter had taken over the family tableware business after the war and made the company's reputation in the fifties with the fashion-orientated Stylecraft ranges that he had himself designed. By 1960, the company was known as the most innovative producer of tableware in Britain, but Roy Midwinter realised that he would now have to produce something different if he was to maintain this hard-won position, and so he approached David Queensberry to design their new range.

Midwinter and Queensberry shared not only a commitment to modern design but also the view that it should be possible to produce a distinctively British contemporary style. The "Fine" shape that resulted from this collaboration in 1962 was an attempt to do just this; its basic milk-churn shape had clean modern lines but could also be related to similar eighteenth-century precedents. Fine was a runaway success in this period, something which took even Midwinter by surprise, with demand outstripping supply. The simple cylindrical shape set the tone for tableware design in the mid-sixties and, before long, almost every major producer had brought out a churn-shaped copy. Queensberry also designed the most

Midwinter's Trend was the first design to combine pottery with a non-stick coating. Unfortunately, the idea was rather in advance of the technology and the non-stick did not always stay stuck to the dishes

successful of the first patterns on the shape – Queensberry Stripe. He claims it took him only half an hour with some chalk to produce the lithographic plate from which the first transfers were made.

Queensberry designed two further shapes for Midwinter, although neither ever matched the sales of Fine. The first, Trend, produced in 1965, was an oven-to-table ware, revolutionary in that it was the first time that a non-stick lining had been applied to a ceramic surface. Unfortunately, ambition had rather overtaken the state of the technology: the Fluon lining had an unfortunate tendency to peel off, which limited the success of the range. A particularly recalcitrant shipment to Canada prompted the pithy telex in return, "Fluon. Flewoff". The next venture, in 1968, was the MQ2 shape (the idea being that "Fine", the first Midwinter-Queensberry collaboration, had been MQ1). Again, a very distinctive basic shape was used, in this case derived from the shape of a laboratory retort flask, upright for the coffeepot, inverted for bowls, cups and serving dishes. It failed, however, to emulate the success of its illustrious predecessor, mainly as a result of financial problems at Midwinter, and died an early death when the firm merged with J&G Meakin later the same year – the combined firm then became part of the Wedgwood group.

Over the same period, David Queensberry also undertook some design work in cut crystal for the manufacturer Webb Corbett, which later became part of Royal Doulton. The company wanted to produce a more modern range, but the crystal had to be cut rather than plain – cutting disguises flaws in the glass as well as bringing out the refractive qualities – so David Queensberry produced a range of modern geometric treatments which received a great deal of favourable publicity and acclaim when they won the Design Council's "Duke of Edinburgh Award for Elegant Design" for 1963.

Meanwhile, in the same year at the Royal College, David Queensberry had taken on a new student by the name of Martin Hunt. The department was still in the process of change and Hunt was one of the last to be subjected to an industry-orientated regime, but in his case the discipline represented a turning point in his career. Like David Queensberry, Hunt's original training had been as a studio potter, but after his arrival at the Royal College, Hunt says that he began to question whether the handcraft approach was either the most interesting or the most skilful: "From the first days at the college I became fascinated by a whole new craft: wonderful plaster of Paris moulds which clicked together perfectly, modelled surfaces that were so pure

Right, far right and below: The idea behind David Queensberry's award-winning designs for Webb Corbett was to modernise the image of cut crystal by using simple geometric patterns on modern forms. It was one of the first significant modern designs in British crystal

they would show any defects arising from lack of skill." Hunt set about trying to master this new craft.

Indeed, by the end of his time at the RCA, he had become so intrigued by the possibilities of this new approach that for a while he considered becoming a consultant designer in industry. He spent some time in his final year producing more general industrial design projects, and even went to interviews at companies like Ford. "I thought that it would be fun going into a completely new world of product design – Hotpoint washing machines as well as cars – I really knew very little about it."

What prevented his career taking this direction was an offer from David Queensberry, who suggested that, after Martin's graduation, they go into partnership. Queensberry reasoned that he was at that time receiving enough offers of work to keep both of them busy and provide a reasonably comfortable living. Queensberry knew that he had the contacts, but he also recognised Hunt's talents: "He was brilliant. Far better than me or, for that matter, many other designers I had come into contact with." For his part, Hunt liked the idea of a smaller, more intimate way of working where he would be meeting the clients rather than working as an invisible backroom boy in a larger company, and so Queensberry Hunt was created in 1966.

These simple pieces in red polished clay from Martin Hunt's degree show won the Royal College of Art prize for three-dimensional design on his graduation in 1966

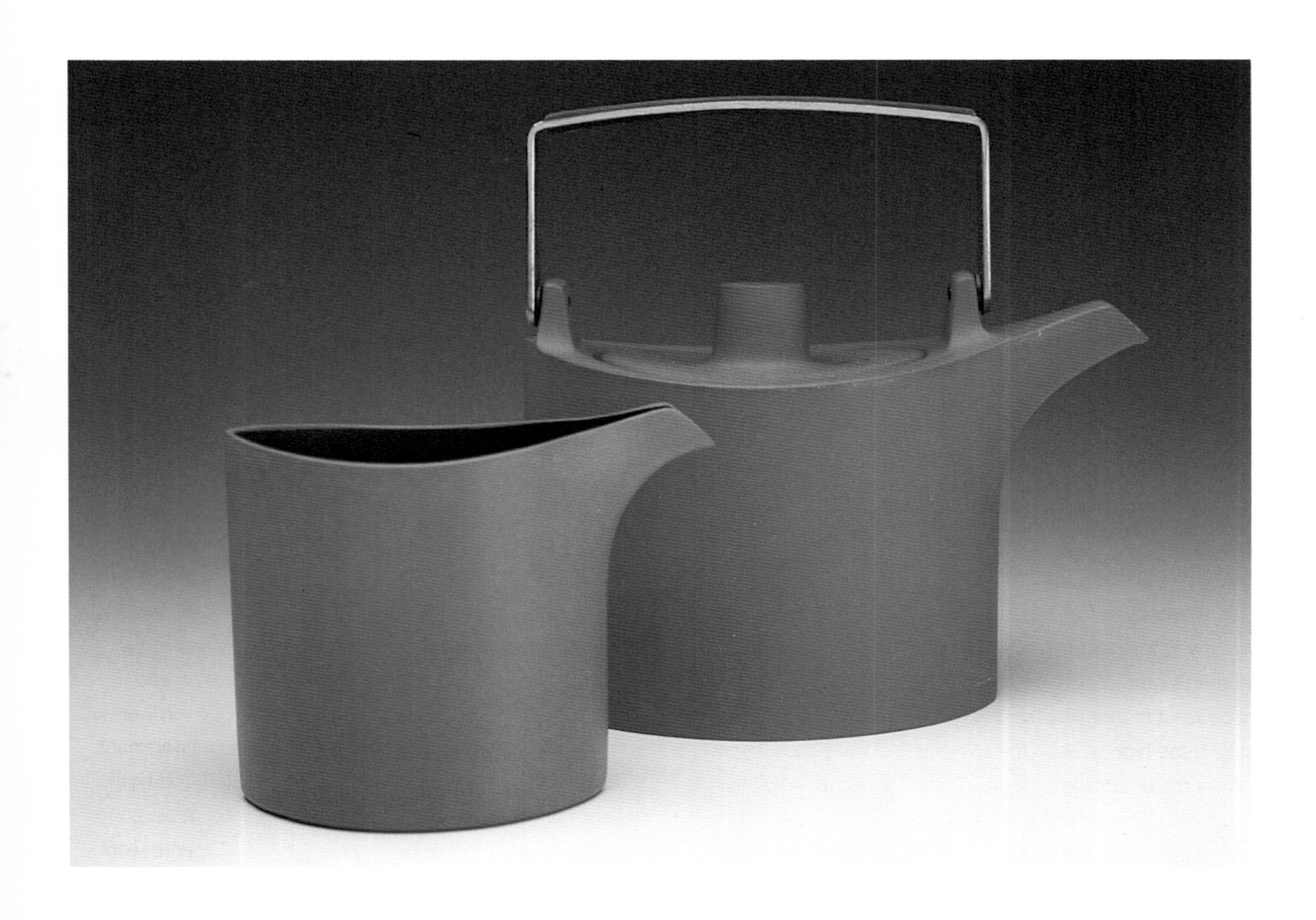

Designed by Martin Hunt together with James Kirkwood, these lamps were sold mainly through Habitat. They won a Design Council award in 1971

Although the combination of Queensberry's knowledge of the industry with both their design abilities made a partnership an obvious course, there were few precedents at the time for such a move. What freelance designers there were in the ceramics industry often worked alone, and the idea of a collective manner of working was completely new, but then the same was true in almost every other field, as design consultancy was only just coming into existence in Britain. Indeed in 1966 there were only five or six consultancies of any size, and most of which, like Queensberry Hunt, had been formed in the early sixties. Martin Hunt remembers the whole industry working on a very different scale in those days: "It was a tiny little pool – anybody who was doing anything was very well known to each other."

At the beginning, this way of working undoubtedly had advantages for Queensberry Hunt; some of their first work was for products which were sold through Terence Conran's new venture Habitat. The shop was a revelation because it meant that modern designs could actually be sold in the high street. One of Habitat's first china ranges (and a major success for them) was David Queensberry's Midwinter "Fine", produced as a special line with plain blue banding for the store. It was a major attraction for Habitat's customers, as Terence Conran remembers: "the Midwinter was very, very successful in those early days because it was so simple and so straightforward." Another of the designs on sale in this early period was a range of very orange light-fittings, designed by Martin Hunt in conjunction with James Kirkwood, a fellow student from the RCA. These fittings were in fact so successful that they won a Design Council award for the pair in 1971.

From this time on, as Terence Conran remembers, Queensberry Hunt had a continuing association with Habitat: "Gradually, during the development of Habitat, someone from Queensberry Hunt was always ringing up and saying, 'look, we've found a pottery who can do this or that and could we come up with an idea for this for you?'".

The commercial pressure for survival did not weigh too heavily on Queensberry Hunt, since both partners were still very much sheltered by their association with the Royal College. David Queensberry was still a professor, and Martin Hunt, who had been taken on by the department as a tutor, eventually became head of the Glass Department. The college encouraged outside work by staff, and both partners saw the presence of Queensberry Hunt as a genuine asset to the college. It meant that students were

One of Queensberry Hunt's earliest designs for Habitat, introduced in 1971, this range also marked the start of the partnership's collaboration with Henry Watson's Pottery

able to draw on the experience and talents of practising industrial designers who were on hand in the department every day, and the partnership could even occasionally provide work for students.

But the experience of working within the college also undoubtedly had a reciprocal effect in that it reinforced both partners' connection with and interest in studio ceramics. The ceramic industry is very different from most others, where there are sharp divisions between craft practice and industrial design. These distinctions are not as obvious in pottery, and working within the very varied environment of a teaching department strengthened the partnership's connection with craft practice.

Queensberry found that studio work provided inspiration not only for his design students but also in his own work: "To this day I still think that the finest achievements in ceramics in the twentieth century do not come from industry." He had maintained an interest in studio pottery since his early days at Central, and collected the work of such leading figures such as Bernard Leach and Hamada in the fifties: "most of my children's school fees have been paid by selling pieces of pottery that I bought twenty or thirty years ago and that have mercifully become quite valuable." Even now, Queensberry still has a considerable collection and is heavily involved in promoting exhibitions of studio work.

However, both Queensberry and Hunt would argue that studio pottery has had a far more fundamental impact on their designs than any mere "inspiration" could have been. In a way that is very unusual in mass production, their work for industry has numerous points of reference in craft practice and studio pottery. This is in part due to the fact that both men originally studied as studio potters. The craft approach that this background fosters has obviously given them a very close relationship with the materials with that they work, as Martin Hunt explains: "I started out as a potter. I've been unadventurous and stayed with the material. It's a question of feeling at home with one's craft."

Occasionally, this studio training has made a direct impact on their designs. For example, Shape 44, a dinnerware design which Martin Hunt developed for the Danish company Bing & Grøndahl, was produced with a tenmoku glaze – a traditional Japanese technique. The brown glaze resulted in very beautiful but highly variable effects when fired, however, Bing & Grøndahl never put the design into production because they felt that it would be rather difficult to market. They suspected that prospective purchasers would not be particularly interested in the studio aesthetic of the randomness of firing, and instead would sort through pieces in the shop in order to acquire a matching set.

Craft has also played an important role in Queensberry Hunt's design methods; the degree of skill and detail which they put into modelmaking has few parallels in the design industry. Modelling has always been a central skill in the ceramics industry, but Martin Hunt in particular saw it as a way in which he could use his craft skills to improve the general standard of industrial products. "The design of the sixties was undemanding of modelmaking, and consequently industry lost some of the skills. It seemed obvious to me that if I intended to control the quality of my designs, in most cases, I would have to make the master models myself."

Beyond the influence of studio pottery in the craft techniques which Queensberry Hunt employ in design, Martin Hunt believes that what they produce is at times as innovative as studio pottery, because their technical knowledge and design skills allow them to develop ideas and techniques that are genuinely new. According to Hunt: "We may be searching for a classicism which enables our customers to feel comfortable, but within the actual content of the design there may be quiet details, new details that artist potters have not discovered. We can discover or rediscover them and put them into mass-produced pottery ahead of artist potters".

As well as providing artistic input and inspiration, the studio environment of the Royal College also provided Queensberry Hunt with the facilities for testing glazes and bodies, and a great deal of technical experimentation went into some of their work. But despite these advantages, it became increasingly clear that the partnership was outgrowing the college. The need for a full-time secretary and a bookkeeper became apparent as the partnership grew in size, and as the quantity of work increased, more designers and modelmakers had been taken on. These included John Horler, a refugee from automotive design, and Robin Levien; both were later to become partners. As a result of this expansion, Queensberry Hunt moved from the Royal College into its own premises in 1980, although both David Queensberry and Martin Hunt continued to teach at the college for several years. For them, the real period of expansion began from this time, since the additional pressure of supporting staff and premises served to make the partnership even more determined. As David Queensberry puts it, "nothing focuses your mind more than survival."

Chapter Two

Design in a cold climate

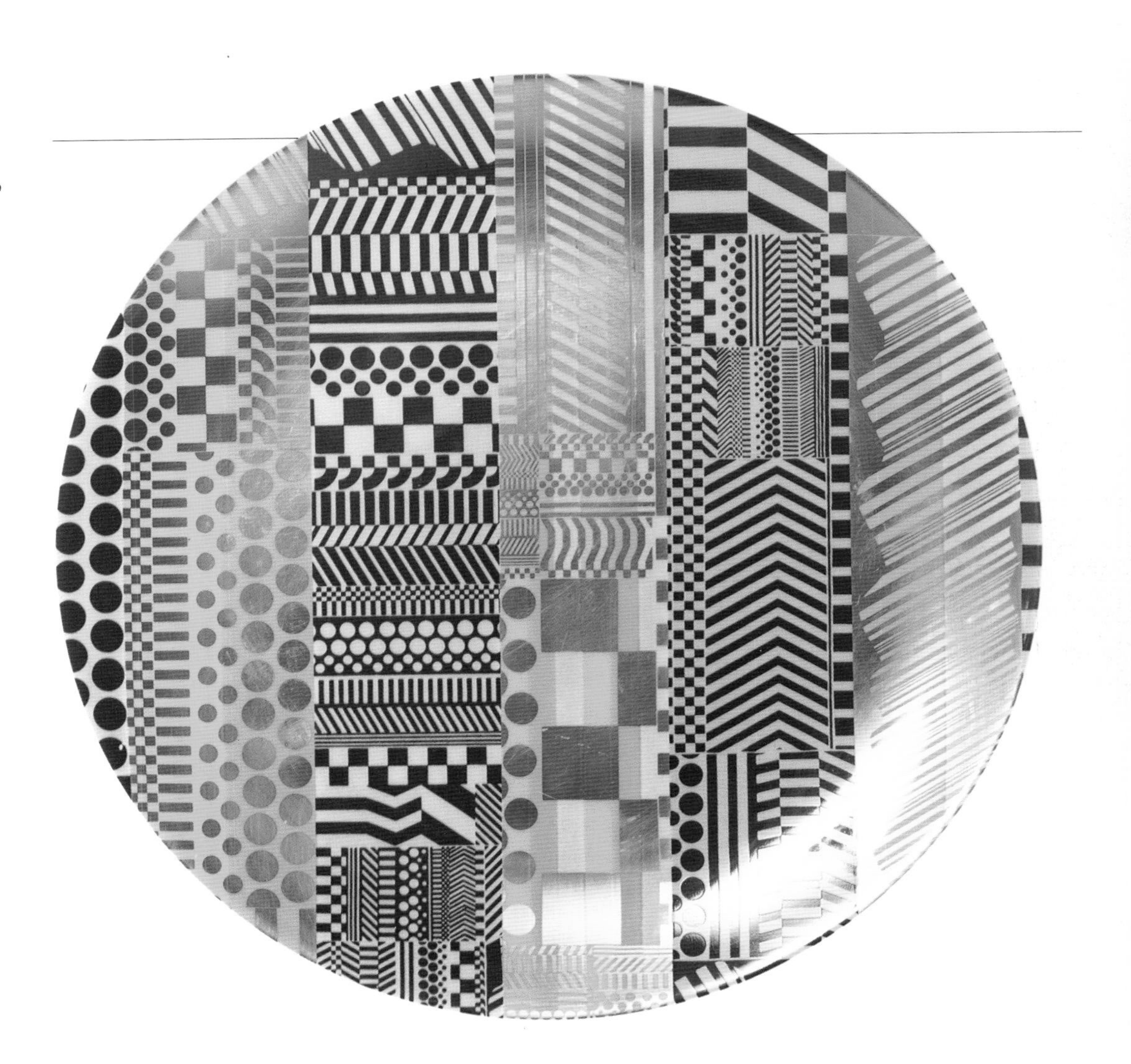

David Queensberry persuaded Wedgwood to produce these plates of Eduardo Paolozzi's. The designs were developed by Brian Cour in the Queensberry Hunt studio

Although Martin Hunt won the Rosenthal Young Designer Award for these designs in 1967, they were not in fact produced by the company until a number of years later

Even while based within the Royal College, Queensberry Hunt's work had not been confined to producing smaller-scale designs for retailers such as Habitat, although these did provide a regular source of design work. The partners had also been employed by a few companies who were completely committed to producing contemporary design of a very high calibre. Given the limited amount of modern tableware which actually gets into production, Queensberry Hunt were fortunate in the ease with which they were able to find manufacturers prepared to put their kind of work into production.

In the early days of the partnership while David Queensberry was still working for Midwinter, one of Martin Hunt's first jobs had been for the influential German company Rosenthal. As well as being known for the quality of their work with ceramic designers such as Tapio Wirkkala and Timo Sarpeneva, Rosenthal also had a reputation for the forceful promotion of modern design. Martin Hunt's work for them were the result of his winning the Rosenthal "Young Designers Competition" in the year following his graduation. Although the designs that he was then commissioned to produce for the company took a long time to come into production, he still feels that the experience of working with a company dedicated to producing contemporary design of the highest quality was an invaluable education. "I had the experience of being exposed to really high-calibre people, both technically and in terms of design motivation." It was a particularly inspiring period for Hunt because the Rosenthal studios excelled in modelmaking, an expertise that he was very keen to develop. The technical accomplishment of the Rosenthal modellers showed the very high level which these skills could attain.

Although the work for Rosenthal was an object lesson in how the highest standards might be achieved by a company with a total commitment to the principles of modern design, the partnership, and Martin Hunt in particular, got far more recognition from the work which they produced for the Danish company Bing & Grøndahl. Despite being a long-established company whose sales and success had come from their more traditional products, Bing & Grøndahl were still determined to remain in the vanguard of modern design. Again, it was the degree of the company's interest in and commitment to developments in modern design that surprised Martin Hunt when he visited the company in Copenhagen. "For all that I was a designer and tutor at the RCA, I came away chastened – ideas on current art, architecture and design

Delfi and Shape 44 were two of the designs which Martin Hunt developed for Bing & Grøndahl in the mid-seventies. Delfi, on the left, had a pattern by the Swedish studio potter, Carl-Harry Stålhane

kept cropping up in factory meetings, and they had usually managed to see an exhibition in London or read an article in English that I had not yet managed to get to."

The initial contact with Bing & Grøndahl had come about partly as a result of Queensberry Hunt's relationship with the RCA and partly with the aid of the Design Council, which in those days was taking a far more active role in helping the (far fewer) British designers obtain work. A deputation from Bing & Grøndahl had come to Britain under the auspices of the Council, and one of the visits arranged was to Queensberry Hunt and the Royal College. (The visit also resulted in Elizabeth Fritsch, then a recent graduate of the course, working as an artist in residence at the company.) The initial invitation to work for Bing & Grøndahl was completely speculative and appears, now, to have been an astonishingly casual arrangement – an open-ended suggestion that the partnership come up with a few designs. Although in retrospect, he feels that "we would never do that amount of work now with no advances or anything," Martin Hunt, nevertheless, travelled over to Copenhagen a few months later with some models and designs for three dinnerware services and the "Tea for One". To his surprise, all of the designs were immediately accepted. "We had never had that sort of reaction before – we hadn't even had a brief and they just set about producing it all."

Of the three tableware designs that Bing & Grøndahl produced, the most successful and perhaps the one with the most enduring appeal is Delfi, a pure rounded shape with a blue hand-painted decoration designed by the Swedish studio ceramist Carl-Harry Stålhane. The design undoubtedly belongs to the tradition of functional but elegant Scandinavian design, however, its simple form also owes a great deal to Hunt's enduring fascination with the perfectibility of the smooth surface possible in mass-produced porcelain. His preference for using materials in this way comes from both his background as a potter and from the broader craft tradition: "I look for those qualities which are expressive of the best of the material. One looks at the archetype materials: bone china, hard paste porcelain etc., and asks 'How can we get the best from them?' To use them to imitate other materials would be to misuse them". His involvement with the precise characteristics of porcelain is also reflected in more subtle details, such as the curve in the footwell of the saucer which holds the cup in place. The particular production methods of the material meant that this would not have been possible in anything other than porcelain.

The Tea for One was probably the most successful of all Martin Hunt's designs for Bing & Grøndahl

This set of nesting bowls was one of many designs which Martin Hunt did for Bing & Grøndahl

The "Tea for One" set, although never sold in Britain, proved to be popular in Europe and America, probably because its variety of decorations could appeal to traditional as well as more modern tastes. The packaging for this particular product also featured a shadowy picture of Martin Hunt in a designer-as-star mode (and as a result, he was even recognised in an American shopping mall). It is rare for Queensberry Hunt to be promoted in so public a fashion with their designs; while their work is always credited to the individual designer as well to as the group, they have still remained relatively anonymous. "We would never be part of the designer/superstar scene, nor would we want to be. To fulfil those requirements, the type of design that you have to do is not what we believe in and we clearly understand that." This attitude stems partially from a determination to produce designs for the mass market: something which can be easily manufactured and which sells can only be more subtly innovative than the sort of design which makes headlines.

It is symptomatic of the lack of innovation and design culture in the British pottery industry that, even in their early days, so many of the partnership's commissions came from abroad. Queensberry Hunt worked for only one company in Britain with a similar attitude to modern design, Hornsea Pottery in Yorkshire. The firm had been set up in 1946 by Desmond and Colin Rawson, two brothers who had had no previous experience of the pottery industry, but had decided to start up on their own anyway. The business was run with a single-minded dedication to perfection as Colin Rawson remembers: "We cared about everything being as right as possible – even in the factory, the placing of a light switch that made things look orderly."

This attitude obviously included the design of Hornsea's products, and this was what made working for them such a salutary experience. Both Colin and Desmond Rawson had been deeply interested in modern design since the early days of their pottery, however, they couldn't really see the point of employing designers if, as is so often the case, successive alterations which occurred during the design process left the original design virtually unrecognisable. Colin Rawson, in particular, felt that this attention to detail was important because the distinctive character of Queensberry Hunt's designs was of a kind that could be very easily compromised by poor workmanship: "The thing that I remember most about Martin and the Queensberry Hunt team is that there would be some little detail in the design that was special to them. It could be beading around the handle, or the type of knobs, but they always

Produced in 1974, Contrast was Hornsea's best-selling range for over twelve years, and was the first of Martin Hunt's three designs for the company to win a Design Council Award

produced something that stood out against other designs." Details such as the layered ridges of Concept could easily have been softened almost to the point of extinction in the production process, and so to guard against this, Colin Rawson ensured that the design which finally resulted remained as close as possible to the designer's original intentions. His concerns extended to touring the factory every day before the employees arrived and work started; he would then be sure that changes had not been made on the shop floor without his knowledge. As Martin Hunt recollects, he took in every detail: "When the first trials of the Concept shape were being made, on a desk in this immaculate, tidy office there was a row of plain pots. Their right-hand man was a chap called Mike Walker, who was responsible for getting a lot of jobs into production. He was their first employee at the age of sixteen in the shed, and he'd grown up with them. Colin said to me, 'Look at these bloody lids.' Mike had sponged the lids slightly too much, and there was a little bit of a slack fit. Colin said, 'Look at that, that's the one I did myself and these are the ones that Mike's done. He's been with us since he was sixteen and he still doesn't understand.'"

Hornsea had originally made contact with Queensberry Hunt, again through the agency of the Design Council, because they needed a range that could be made at their new factory which was about to open in Lancaster, a project which eventually became Contrast. Martin Hunt came up with a very simple and cylindrical shape which was at least partly inspired by the technical trials that Colin Rawson had been undertaking at the pottery. One of the advantages of being self-taught in the industry was a certain open-mindedness, and from the earliest days of the Hornsea Pottery Rawson had been prepared to experiment with ideas that more traditional firms would never have even bothered to consider. When Queensberry Hunt first came to work for the company, he had been experimenting for some time with the idea of polishing a very hard ceramic surface ("vitrified" – fired so that the body becomes non-porous), producing a smooth resistant surface without glazing. The effect which resulted was startlingly different from anything else then on the market, and by the time that Contrast was being designed, Hornsea had perfected this technique so that it could be used in industrial production.

Just as Hunt's designs for Bing & Grøndahl drew on the gloss and whiteness of the porcelain, so Contrast emphasised the particular qualities of the vitrified body. The straight-sided shape underlined the solidity of the

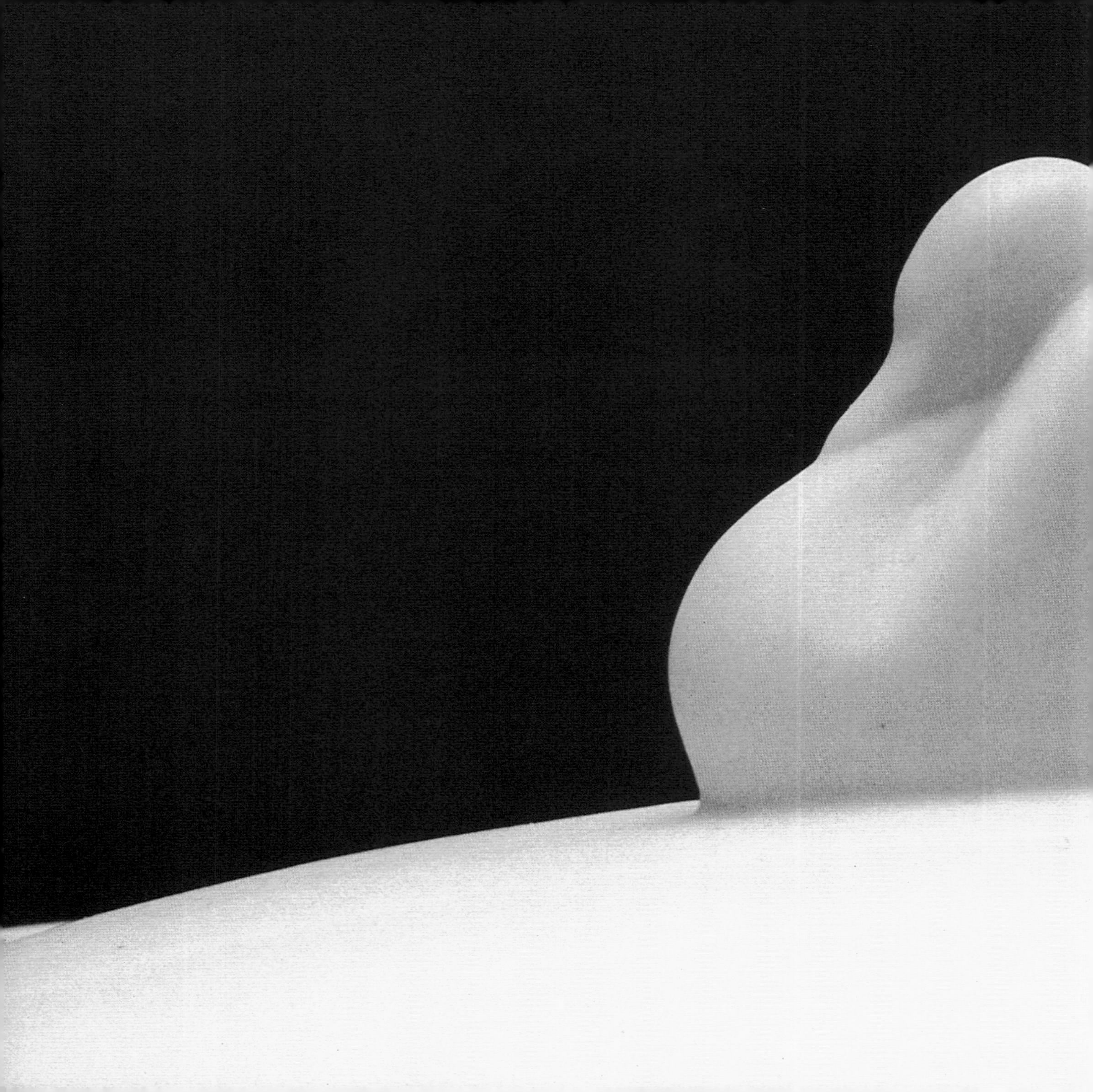

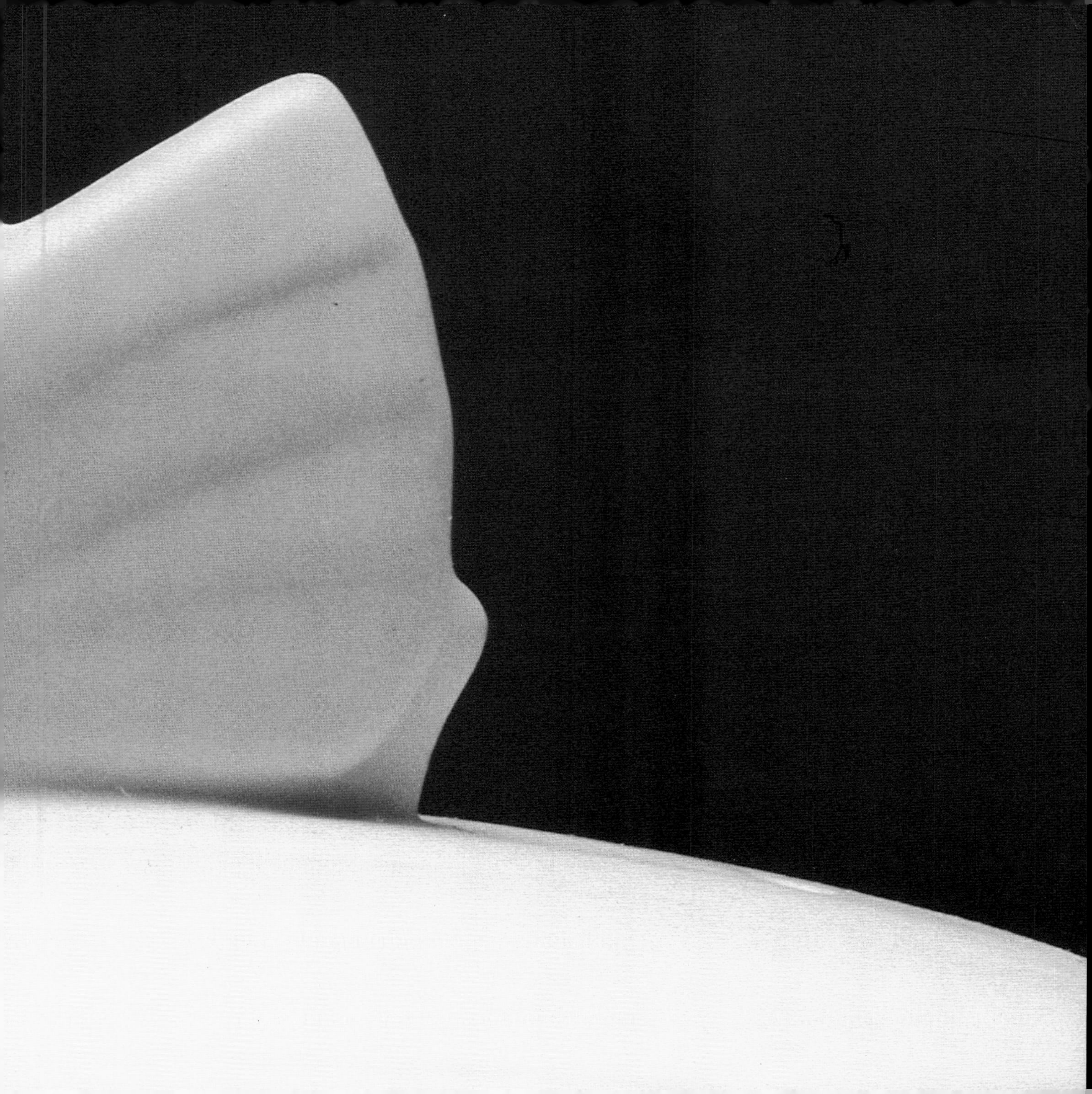

Previous page, left and opposite: Concept, Martin Hunt's next design for Hornsea, was intended to be a more formal design than its predecessor. The finely-modelled design required a very high standard of potting to be successful

material and the stonelike finish, while the band of glaze contrasted with both the unglazed polished surface and the deep chocolate-brown colour of the body.

The next shape that Hunt produced for Hornsea, Concept, also relied on the qualities of the polishing technique for its effect. However, the intention here was to make a very different style of design from Contrast with a more refined look which could sell alongside bone china. The polishing technique was again pre-eminent, but was employed for a very different effect. The delicate gradations which form the main feature of Concept would have been almost obliterated had it been glazed, but polishing left the details sharp on the surface. In keeping with the finer potting and more delicate nature of the design, the contrast between the glazed areas – here in the centre of the "ripples" – and the polished body is more subtle, as is the lighter colour of the body. But the most distinctive feature of Concept is the swan which forms the knob on a number of the pieces. It was the kind of quirky detail which, for Colin Rawson, gave Queensberry Hunt's designs their particular personality. Exactly how such a design feature comes about is almost impossible even for its designer to define: "I rationalise it by comparing the curves to the ripples formed by a pebble in a pond, and all those post-rationalisations did seem to fit – there is a sort of logic to the swan."

Both designs were enormously successful: Contrast kept its place as Hornsea's best-selling range for over twelve years, while Concept was particularly popular overseas, especially in America and Scandinavia and so opened up new export markets for the company. The third range that Martin Hunt designed for Hornsea, Ebony, achieved a more modest success. Like the two previous designs, Ebony built on the results of Colin Rawson's technical experimentation, but this time he had managed to recreate a material known to the Romans as *terra sigillata*. Pots were coated in a coloured clay suspension composed of extremely fine particles which during the firing, fuse into a smooth impervious skin. It is difficult to say why this range was less successful than its predecessors – accounting for why a one range succeeds while another fails is always an inexact science. Although Colin Rawson felt that Ebony's relative lack of success ultimately stemmed from marketing mistakes rather than any intrinsic problem with the design, Martin Hunt believes that the brief and design may have failed to take account of changes which had occurred since the success of Contrast; perhaps Ebony had been too severely modern for the market at the time.

Although it too won a Design Council Award, Concord never matched the commercial success of Concept and Contrast. Opposite: Colin Rawson was very interested in technical innovation at Hornsea, and Cirrus, on Concept, was one of the results of his experiments

Another remarkable thing about the work with Hornsea is that each of the three ranges that Martin Hunt designed won a Design Council award. A complete belief in the standards of the Design Council was an integral part of the Rawson brothers' dedication to good design, and Hornsea was one of the few potteries to actively work towards Design Council acceptance. The company also undertook to put into full production only those designs that had been approved by the Council. As Hunt recalls: "Nothing was too much trouble – they were the absolute opposite to the cynical Stoke on Trent lot." It was this unquestioning faith in good design that, in Queensberry Hunt's eyes, set Hornsea apart from the rest of the industry in Britain. The tragedy is of course that such an attitude does not guarantee the commercial success of products, and when times got harder Hornsea suffered financial difficulties and was eventually taken under new management.

However, for Martin Hunt this attitude was more than just a shared passion, it was also one of the fundamental ingredients for producing good design. "It was the kind of semi-panic level that went on at Hornsea that was so good because everybody would do anything. It could become a real hothouse in a way because no one would stop until the job was done. That was a thrill because it carries you along, and I think that in a way doing good work comes out of a spirit, a team of people that really want to do it."

Finding other companies in Britain that have this kind of ethos or even an interest in modern design is a problem which has faced Queensberry Hunt since their work with Hornsea. It also underlines just how fortunate they had been with their earlier commissions. Part of the problem is that, since the 1960s, the industry in Britain has become more and more centralised, as larger firms such as Wedgwood, Royal Worcester and Doulton have bought up the smaller independent manufacturers such as Susie Cooper, Midwinter, Meakin and many more. Unfortunately, it had been precisely these smaller firms that were most prepared to experiment with modern design. As the larger firms concentrated on the mass market, the conglomerates increased in size, and opportunities for introducing more innovative designs gradually disappeared.

The few independent potteries which did survive faced a considerable struggle and became less and less able or willing to invest in risky modern design. Queensberry Hunt ceased to work for Hornsea when the company ran into financial difficulties and was taken over. Poole Pottery, for whom Queensberry Hunt also produced a number of designs, was a further example of a small company which

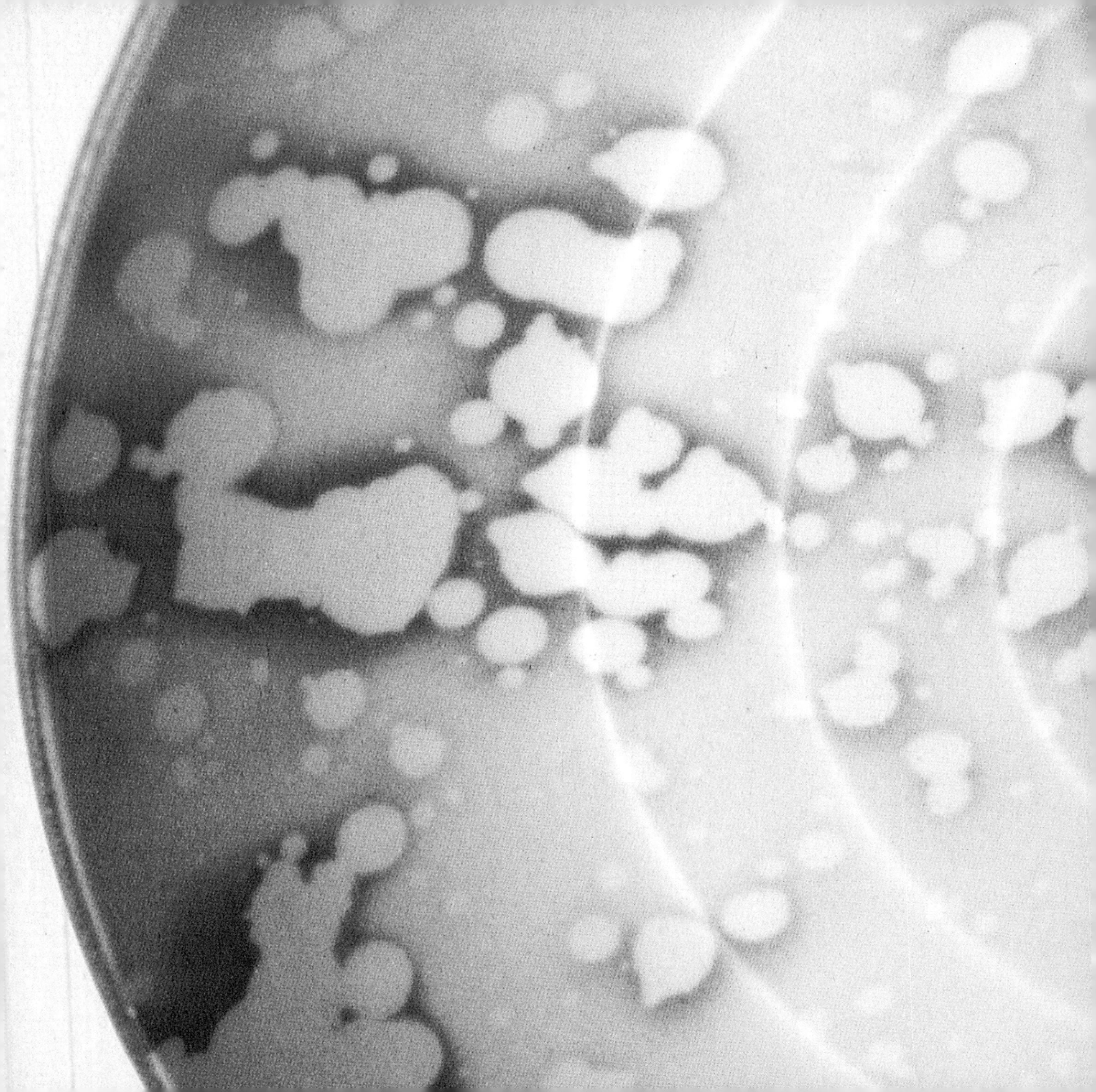

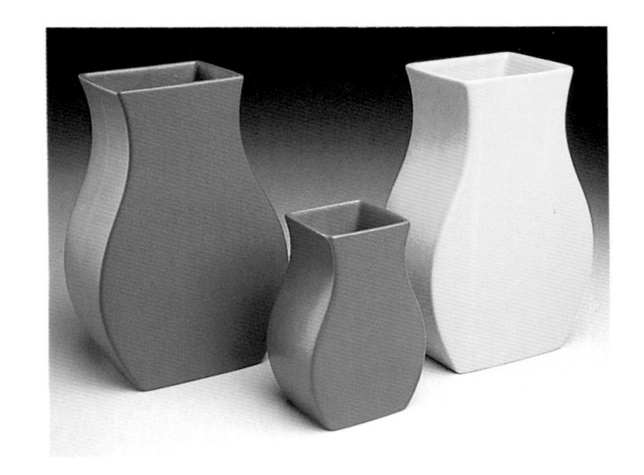

eventually abandoned the production of contemporary work. Both before and after the Second World War, Poole had acquired a reputation for producing simple but innovative designs, and their very plain shapes with distinctive two-tone eggshell glazes became the pottery's trademark. In the early eighties, Queensberry Hunt were responsible for a number of their designs, and John Horler worked closely with the company in developing some very successful small vases and giftware, as well as two complete tableware ranges: Flair and Astral. These restrained, shape-based designs fitted in well with Poole's tradition of simple modern design. However, Queensberry Hunt's connection with Poole ended when, as a response to the general depression of the mid-eighties, the company told Queensberry Hunt that their design budget was to be drastically reduced. Poole's parent holding company had decided that design of this standard was not essential, and was a luxury that they could no longer afford.

This kind of attitude underlines another difficulty faced by Queensberry Hunt within the British context. The decline of smaller firms is not the merely result of the restructuring of industry. Another effect is that large companies are now seldom run by people with any real interest in their product or its design. Martin Hunt explains: "Much of the industry is dominated by people who have very little knowledge of how things are made. The owner-manufacturer has been replaced by "corporate man". He's probably got a degree in accountancy or has come up through sales." As a result of this, companies have little passion for the product or interest in innovation. The master potter like Colin Rawson has become a thing of the past. It was the devotion to the product and readiness to take risks which made working with Hornsea such a rewarding experience for Queensberry Hunt and Martin Hunt in particular.

The attitude which Queensberry Hunt found in working for companies such as Rosenthal, Bing & Grøndahl and Hornsea contrasts markedly with their experiences in the large British conglomerates. For a number of years, Queensberry Hunt had a consultancy agreement with the Wedgwood group and produced a considerable number of designs for them. While some of the designs were good, neither party looks on the experience as having been very rewarding, and what is even more surprisingly, none of the designs which resulted from this association with Wedgwood was particularly successful. Martin Hunt candidly admits that "not everything can be a best-seller", and the success or failure of individual products is in any case always difficult to predict.

Left: Cello vases for Poole, designed by John Horler. Right and below: Two of Queensberry Hunt's designs for Poole; Flair tableware and stacking vases. The vases were rejected by the Design Council on the grounds that the colours were "too controversial", that is, they were not black and white

An example of the many different factors which can affect the success of a range is the Lyndhurst shape which Queensberry Hunt developed for Wedgwood's American market. The original brief was to produce a shape in a cream-coloured body which, although considerably cheaper, would be able to compete with bone china in terms of style and delicacy. However, a series of production factors conspired to make the final product almost as expensive as bone china itself, and as a result, the new range made little impact on the market. Sir Arthur Bryan, the former Chairman of the Wedgwood Group who had been responsible for initially engaging Queensberry Hunt, provides the following analysis: "The thing that made Lyndhurst a spectacular failure was the fact that it was in a non-bone china cream body but it was the same price as bone china. Every American buying dinnerware wants bone china from Wedgwood."

Wedgwood itself is quite prepared to concede that, in this case, the marketing rather than the shape was at fault. However, it is also to some extent true that Queensberry Hunt's work for Wedgwood was never wholly successful because the partnership was committed to a type of modern design that was not appropriate for the company, and they had been over-optimistic in trying to place it there.

Coalport hexagonal giftware (right) and Lyndhurst tableware (far right), both for Wedgwood. Although the Coalport range was unsuccessful for Wedgwood, the designs were subsequently bought back by Queensberry Hunt and resold to America, where they fared considerably better

One range of giftware produced for the company's Coalport subsidiary was what David Queensberry calls "a good example of something that Queensberry Hunt did which was fundamentally stupid". Based on a twisted hexagon, it was a very strong design, but far too modern for the company and was unlikely appeal to the sort of customers who frequented Wedgwood shops. The group was perhaps blinded to this fact by their own enthusiasm for the style. David Queensberry believes that they are unlikely to repeat this kind of mistake: "As you get older and more experienced, you should reduce the chances of making this sort of blunder. You always need to ask the question, 'Is this company right for this design?'".

All of the partners have their own views on why various products developed in conjunction with Wedgwood were not the successes that they might have been; it might have been the marketing, the lack of belief in modern design or the fact that Queensberry Hunt did not design in the right idiom for the company. One consideration which they believe has a major effect on the quality of design is their relationship with the client. With Wedgwood, a major problem was that their consultancy agreement was very open-ended and no one in the company had a clear idea of what they wanted Queensberry Hunt to produce for them: "Nobody was coming back at us saying, 'This is what we want; this is what we do like; this is what we don't like,' and I think that funnily enough, one needs some sort of reaction and feedback for the best work to happen."

There was also a fundamental problem which was only recognised with hindsight: Wedgwood was simply a very different company from Queensberry Hunt, with very different design goals. "There was a kind of cultural mismatch between Wedgwood and ourselves. The successful pieces of work that the earthenware division have produced since our relationship have been mainly repro-style products. You can't knock it – it's perfectly positioned in the market, but it's not our culture. We don't believe in it totally; we don't identify with it; we don't do it."

The absence of a substantial commitment to modern design is hardly unique to the Wedgwood group in Britain. The emphasis is increasingly on traditional styles rather than innovative design, a situation which seems inevitable in an industry dominated by a few large companies. Queensberry recognises the fact that "it is much more difficult to be successful in the mass market with our style of design." As a result, Queensberry Hunt now have very few major clients in Britain, and are forced to work abroad in order to get their kind of design into production.

David Queensberry tried to persuade Wedgwood to reintroduce marbled ceramics, a technique that they had perfected in the eighteenth century. Unfortunately, the project was never put into full production

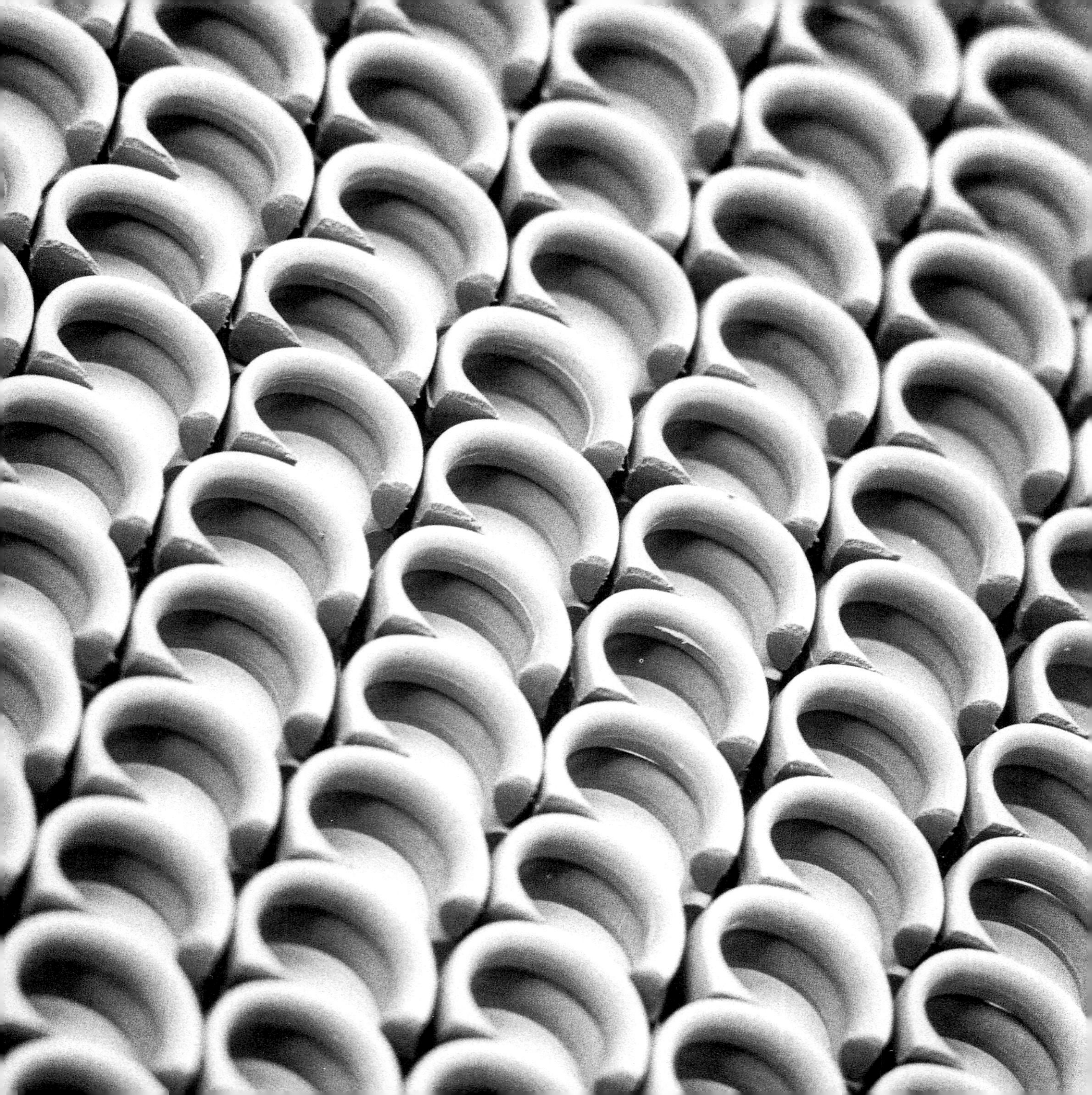

Reshaping the table

Robin Levien's dramatic degree show work was a response to the demands of mass production, using only the simplest methods but at the same time introducing an "existential twist" into each design

One of the intentions behind A-Ware was that it should be consciously rule-breaking; contrary to accepted ideas, in these plant-pot holders, the height of the bases is kept constant, regardless of the size

Few would find it surprising that Queensberry Hunt have increasingly sought to work with companies abroad. It has proved to be only way for the partnership to make the sort of design they wanted and to make it commercially successful. The best example of this is the Trend design, which Queensberry Hunt produced for the German manufacturers Thomas, and which became Europe's best-selling contemporary tableware range during the eighties. The design is almost archetypal Queensberry Hunt in its clean shape and the way in which its character depends on form and surface finish rather than pattern – series of shallow glaze-filled ridges are the signature of the design – and the appeal of the form alone is sufficient to sell the range. It is very rare for tableware to be more popular in plain rather than patterned versions, and yet Trend sold almost 80 per cent in white when it was first launched in 1982; even now, 50 per cent of sales are undecorated.

For Queensberry Hunt, the success of Trend underlines just how much can be achieved when the relationship with the client is right. In contrast with the major British producers, Thomas conformed to their definition of the ideal client as "one whose current products are the sorts of things that you wish that you had already designed yourself," and without a doubt, a similarity of aims and outlook between the two companies has been the most crucial factor in the success of their partnership. As befitted the mass-market subsidiary of Rosenthal, Thomas was dedicated to putting good modern design on the market, and was best known for the designs it had produced in the late sixties. These were quite severe but understated designs, often of Scandinavian inspiration, and sold well in Germany, where consumers were more receptive to modern design than in Britain.

Trend was designed by one of the newer partners in Queensberry Hunt, Robin Levien. Along with the fourth partner, John Horler, he joined in the late seventies after studying at the Royal College of Art. Levien had been a student of David Queensberry in the ceramics department, where his degree show project, an ideologically based range called "A-Ware", had been designed with two other students, Geoff Hollington and Ben Kelly. The collective way of working, despite the radical intentions and "existential twists" of the range, was at least some preparation for work with Queensberry Hunt. While A-Ware was intended for production by the most commonplace mass manufacturing techniques of white slipcasting and clear glazing, it was also deliberately perverse in its appearance, displaying its mould lines openly, and

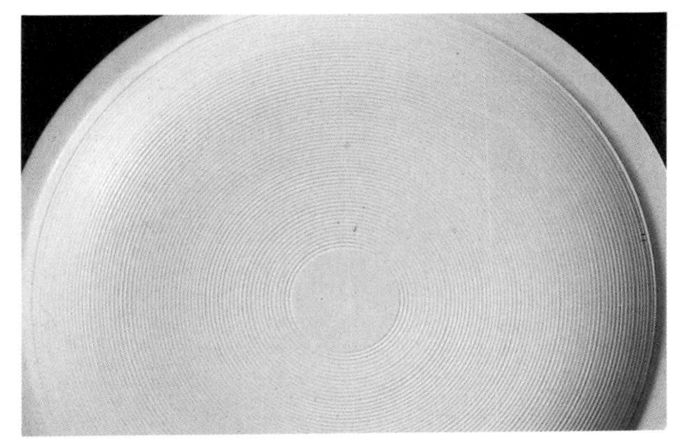

The surface texture of the Trend range makes it simple and at the same time distinctive. In this early model the lines do not yet go to the centre of the plate

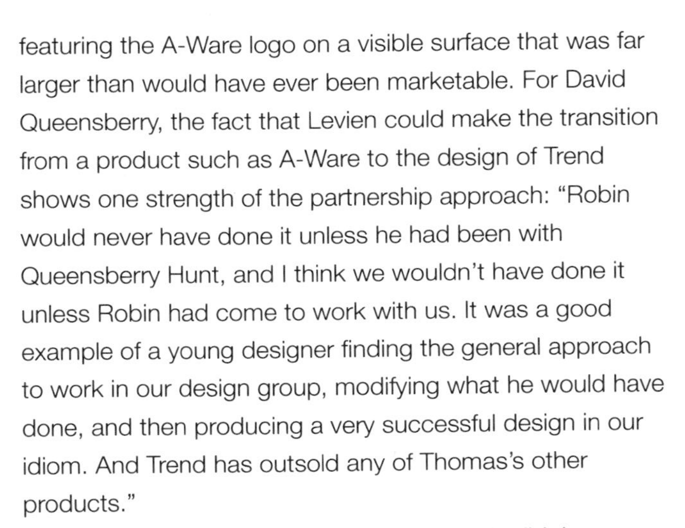

featuring the A-Ware logo on a visible surface that was far larger than would have ever been marketable. For David Queensberry, the fact that Levien could make the transition from a product such as A-Ware to the design of Trend shows one strength of the partnership approach: "Robin would never have done it unless he had been with Queensberry Hunt, and I think we wouldn't have done it unless Robin had come to work with us. It was a good example of a young designer finding the general approach to work in our design group, modifying what he would have done, and then producing a very successful design in our idiom. And Trend has outsold any of Thomas's other products."

However, although Robin Levien ultimately did the detailed design work on Trend, the initial concept had come from David Queensberry. The contact with Thomas had been established because the company was a subsidiary of Rosenthal, with whom Queensberry Hunt had long been associated. David Queensberry had visited the Rosenthal factory as part of his exploration of European ceramic design after joining the Royal College. He became close friends with Philip Rosenthal, the head of the company, and he was asked to join the Rosenthal Jury, an institution which exemplified the missionary zeal of the firm's attitude to design. It was an approach which, to a certain extent, stemmed from Philip Rosenthal's own influence. The jury comprised a selection of the great and the good from the world of art and design who would vet not only proposed Rosenthal and Thomas designs, but also any prospective items for sale in the Rosenthal Studio Shops.

It was typical of David Queensberry's approach that he felt he ought to justify this position with the company by taking on a role that went further than merely approving or rejecting designs and products. When he began to feel that the company's image was losing its appeal, he told them as much. By the end of the seventies, after well over a decade spent on the jury, Queensberry felt that Rosenthal, and in particular their Thomas products, were failing to take into account changing attitudes and more informal eating habits among young people. This was accompanied by another favourite theme of Queensberry Hunt's: the dullness of tableware departments in stores. According to David Queensberry, the importance of tableware is all to do with food and drink, "but going into a store's food department is so much more interesting than looking at china and glass; it ought to be more about food but it is just a wall of white." Queensberry advised Thomas that they should try to convey some of the pleasures of food in the selling and marketing of their tableware. The basic idea was that design should take into account all of these factors and not simply be an exercise in styling, which was what Rosenthal and Thomas's approach had become.

Rosenthal were not entirely sure how they should react to this suggestion, and so asked Queensberry Hunt to develop the idea further. As far as both David Queensberry and Queensberry Hunt were concerned, this did not mean presenting designs for a new tableware range; instead they were more concerned about aspects of food and eating habits. They therefore set about the idea of redefining tableware by looking at food: pasta, for example, represented a new, informal kind of meal. Slides showed the preparation and eating of food, suggestions for marketing and even package design. The idea would be to package a tableware set which contained everything a person might need for pasta – from recipe books to plates and even a pasta machine.

It says something for the conservatism of the tableware industry that this approach, incorporating attitudes and ergonomics, pretty standard stuff for the design of any other product, could be described by Robin Levien as "a radical rethink, a totally unconventional approach to tableware". Nevertheless, before this, the brief for almost any new range had nearly always been couched in the same terms: "it must be easy to make; it must be commercial; it must take pattern," with the proviso that "it must be commercial," comprising the maximum amount of market research that a producer might indulge in. In some respects the reluctance of tableware manufacturers to reconsider their products is understandable; it is perhaps one of the few remaining industries in which neither the methods nor the materials of manufacture have changed fundamentally over the centuries. For that matter, the same might also be said for its products: a Meissen teapot is still as functional today as the Trend model. The result was that, even in companies such as Rosenthal, whose designs were dynamic and modern, an almost formulaic approach to the development of new ranges persisted.

Despite the radical intentions for selling and packaging, Trend eventually became a range of tableware which was not vastly different from many others. However, Queensberry Hunt themselves had always been keen to develop a complete range of tableware. It would have to be a new design, since the idea for food-related sets which they had put forward was not one which would fit in with any of Rosenthal or Thomas's existing ranges, and the sets

Right: The oil and vinegar bottle is one of the quirkier items in the Trend range, designed more as a promotional item than anything else
Below: Since cups, plates and bowls constitue the majority of all sales, Queensberry Hunt was keen to develop a complete range of Trend

The side handle which appears on several Trend pieces was part of the design from the beginning, and is one of the features which make the range casual and comfortable to use

would not sell well unless the basics – cups, plates and bowls – were also available. Some 65 per cent of all tableware sales are plates, cups and saucers, so it was an important consideration for Queensberry Hunt, working for royalties, to ensure that these were part of the design. Thomas, on the other hand, thought that the idea for the pasta set and other food-based sets which followed was limiting – it was felt that they were far too different to be accepted by consumers. Plates and cups were therefore added to the range, and non-Trend items such as recipe books and pasta-makers were dropped until eventually the proposal had evolved from being "totally different to the existing idea of dinner set, tea set, coffee set", into the marketing of tableware through food. But this in fact proved to be a remarkably successful approach, and certainly had some bearing on the design which resulted.

Robin Levien would argue that one innovation their approach produced was a more versatile and appropriate selection of items than was possible under the usual brief. Rethinking the whole approach meant deciding what items were needed rather than starting from the list of items and dimensions with which designers were usually presented (a list which is usually derived entirely from previous ranges). However, the only new product that actually resulted from all this was a single pasta plate in the form of a shallow lipped bowl. While this is undoubtedly useful for eating sloppy foods such as pasta and risotto, and has been a highly successful part of the Trend range, it is not a completely new product, resembling the shallow soup plates that were formerly produced. The design historian Fiona McCarthy described it as: "one of those craftsman potter's supper plates in a new and rather more sophisticated guise". The fact that the idea for the range originated with a pasta set also had an effect on some of the more esoteric pieces produced, such as Parmesan bowls and sauce warmers, but this was more a result of the phenomenal success of the range, which prompted the manufacturer to extend it further and further than a response to changing eating habits.

What was noteworthy about the development of Trend, and at the same time typical of Queensberry Hunt's approach, was the way in which the partnership created their own design opportunities. David Queensberry thinks that the idea was the key to having it accepted: "I had what you might call a basic concept – it was in a sense a tableware 'for all seasons'. We sold it to them on the basis of trying to rethink tableware." Had they approached Thomas with the idea of just a new dinner service, there

would have been little interest; it is selling of a concept which is half of all design work.

The way in which the food and marketing aspects are stressed by all concerned can perhaps obscure other reasons for the ultimate success of Trend. The appeal of the range does not in fact lie in a radical shift in ideas about tableware; indeed, rather the contrary, it is the marked understyling of Trend which makes the range instantly comfortable and familiar, and is the key to its success. It was a very deliberate attempt to produce something that fitted in with more casual and relaxed eating habits. Robin Levien believes that his conception of the range is best expressed by Hugh Casson's remark that good design is "design you feel at ease with". He enlarges on this by ascribing at least part of the range's success to the fact that "sometimes you are designing for somebody else, but I think that part of Trend's success was that in a way we were designing for ourselves, for the way we were living." Certainly the proof of this statement is found in the fact that David Queensberry and Robin Levien both still use the range in their own homes.

The association with Rosenthal and Thomas has been a particularly rewarding one for Queensberry Hunt. The lasting success and popularity of the Trend range has provided the consultancy with not only a continuing stream of work as the range has extended into woodware and cutlery, but also a steady income from the royalties. An additional benefit for the partnership has been the opportunity to work for a company with whom they were in harmony about the nature of good design. The resulting relationship has been sufficiently stable for Queensberry Hunt to produce two further designs for Thomas. Both the Tournee and York ranges, designed by Martin Hunt, are more formal, and therefore aimed at a rather different part of the market from Trend. The success of Trend itself has been so lasting that even after more than a decade, Thomas still sees no need to replace it – the range still forms almost half of their dinnerware sales.

Queensberry Hunt's work over the last quarter century has not, however, been restricted to designing award-winning tableware for well-known companies. A great deal of their design work has been more low key, almost to the point of anonymity, since the beginning of the partnership in the sixties they have designed simple and popular products for shops such as Habitat. Through David Queensberry's early friendship with Terence Conran, Queensberry Hunt have maintained a close relationship with Habitat until Conran's departure from the company,

Opposite: Simple but successful designs developed for Habitat – these ashtrays and stacking candlesticks were produced by Doulton Insulators
Below: Martin Hunt's Roulette tableware was also sold in Habitat – the original design for this had been inspired by the work of Keith Murray

and some of their highest volume products – chicken bricks and candlesticks, plant pots and ashtrays – have been designed for the shop. Although simple, such items can be highly profitable – a single line like a candlestick, if successful, might sell as many 50,000 per year for up to ten years. Terence Conran attributes a considerable part of this not just to Queensberry Hunt's design skills, but also to David Queensberry's commercial acumen: "It's a matter of knowing the market at that particular moment in time. Again, this is what David is good at doing – he's good at being able to spot a mass-market trend."

This business sense is one of the things that sets Queensberry Hunt apart from other product design consultancies. They would work with Habitat in a way quite different from most other firms: suggesting ideas for products and then, if these were accepted, acting as a broker for the ideas, finding a company to produce them and ensuring that the products got into the shops. Some of the items developed in this fashion were done as part of the work with Wedgwood, and were among the more successful results of this partnership. By the early eighties, Queensberry Hunt had already designed two tableware shapes, Bianca and Roulette, which Wedgwood were producing for Habitat. Bianca in particular was very

The turned and sponged ware developed for T G Green, although never sold, was designed to employ the manufacturing techniques which the company had traditionally used to produce their familiar blue-striped Cornish kitchenware

successful and was one of Habitat's best-selling white ranges. When Queensberry Hunt started to consider another shape, however, they were well aware that Habitat's purchasing power alone would not make developing the new shape worthwhile. They therefore approached Sainsbury's, who were then just moving into tableware, and proposed that they share the costs of the new shape, which each shop could then sell in different decorative schemes. When the idea was agreed, Queensberry Hunt arranged for the Wedgwood subsidiary Johnson Brothers to produce the design. By working not only on the designs but also on business ideas in this way, Queensberry Hunt were again able to generate work for themselves which would not have otherwise existed.

Terence Conran believes that a good deal of this entrepreneurial approach is due to David Queensberry himself; "If David had come from an East End background in London rather than the nobility, he would have been a very successful 'fixer'. He's got a real market trader streak in him – something that I have always liked and admired. And he likes all the trappings of business – many designers don't like business but David actually likes the process of of buying and selling things, making deals and making things happen."

This entrepreneurial aspect of the company does not merely consist of smart business sense: as well as getting the right products to the right market, a great many of Queensberry Hunt's ventures also employ their detailed knowledge of ceramic production in order to get things produced at the best quality and the lowest price. Two very successful ranges of Victorian-style candlesticks and plant pots came about when the partnership was approached by Doulton Insulators, a firm which had previously only made electrical components. These were made by turning solid lumps of clay, a method not previously used anywhere else in the industry for making domestic consumer items. Products therefore had to be devised which could be made in this fashion.

The chicken brick, one of the best-selling Queensberry Hunt products in Habitat, was another example of this kind of development. Habitat was already selling a chicken brick, but David Queensberry saw how it might be made more efficiently, and knew of a pottery which already made terracotta where this might be done. As Terence Conran remembers: "We were having the chicken brick made by some other pottery and it was really inefficient. It was thrown and then cut in half with wire. When it was put in the kiln it warped and never fitted together properly, so

Left and right: Designed to compliment country-style kitchens, the Original Suffolk range which Queensberry Hunt designed for Henry Watson's is still a remarkable success over ten years after its launch

David came up with the idea of getting Watson's to make a moulded version which was much more accurate." Martin Hunt redesigned the brick as a single piece which formed both the top and bottom, so that it could be pressed and only one mould would be needed. Not only was the production more accurate, the resulting product cost half what the previous version had.

Work on the brick was done in conjunction with Henry Watson's Pottery, a small family-run enterprise in Suffolk which had had a long association with Queensberry Hunt. Mike Watson, the latest generation of the family to own and run the business, had been at the Royal College when David Queensberry became a professor, and through this contact Martin Hunt had designed some simple ashtrays sold through Habitat, as well as some oven-to-tableware for the pottery in the late sixties. But by the end of the seventies Henry Watson's was facing the problems of being a small company in an industry dominated by firms the size of Wedgwood and Doulton. Their product was good, but their prices made them uncompetitive.

In conjunction with Mike Watson, David Queensberry devised a scheme for firing and decorating their terracotta in one single process. By putting any decoration directly on to the unfired clay, the need for a second firing for decoration was eliminated. A great deal of technical experimentation was required to get this into production, but once the technique was put into operation the savings made were significant.

Queensberry Hunt then designed the product which was to be made in this way, a range of terracotta kitchenware with a logo derived from the 1911 Army and Navy Stores catalogue. Mike Watson was not at first convinced that this would be the salvation of his pottery, "I thought it was crazy – it was really corny. I honestly didn't think it would bale us out of the problems that we were in." In fact Queensberry Hunt's commercial antennae had anticipated exactly the demand for safe, nostalgic styles, and the product has been one of the great success stories of the eighties, selling spectacularly both at home and abroad. In addition, it was yet another business deal that provided Queensberry Hunt not only with royalty income but also a steady stream of work as the product range was expanded. The success of the product has been so great that Henry Watson's have been unable to produce anything else. Concerned that the range might eventually lose momentum, they have tried different, more modern approaches, but the retailers see no reason to sell other variations while the Original Suffolk range is doing so well.

Chapter Four

Design at work

In Tournee, the twisted handles render the simplest and most familiar tableware shapes modern and distinctive

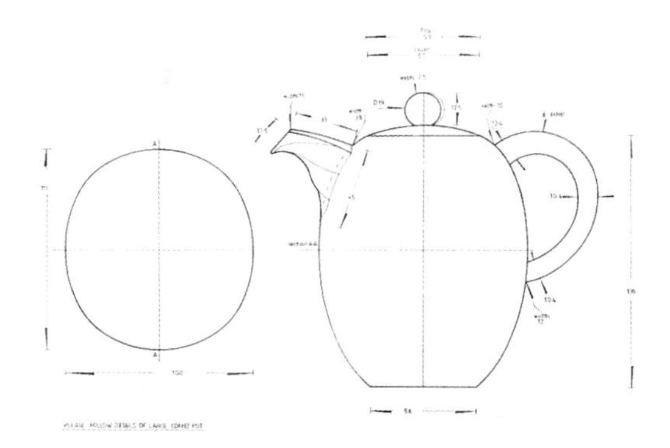

Although Queensberry Hunt are unusual in a number of respects – their entrepreneurial attitude to design and their detailed knowledge of their industry for example – they believe that what defines and differentiates them from other designers and consultancies is their craft background and outlook. Modelmaking, as a way of working, means that their designs develop in a very different way than might otherwise be the case. The fact that Queensberry Hunt's working practices have evolved along these lines reflects in part the influence of Martin Hunt, who had been interested in the craft and discipline of modelmaking since his early studies at the Royal College. As an example of the effect that this approach has had on his own designs, he cites Tournee, his recent work for the firm Thomas. He says of the design's very distinctive twisted handle, that "It's the sort of design which comes out of modelmaking, because designers who are not modelmakers themselves just wouldn't put in the effort to specify something that is going to be so difficult to model. Maybe by designing in a little more complexity one moves the idea into a landscape where it is difficult for them to follow."

The story of how the twist on the Tournee handle came about gives some idea of the processes involved in the development of an idea through modelling. The original concept of the twisted handle came from a sketch, and in order to explore this further, Martin Hunt cast a number of hexagonal rods in silicone rubber. These could be twisted into different spirals, and only when the right profile had been achieved did he actually produce some handles in plaster – each one had to be modelled separately by hand, since the rubber was too flexible to make casts from.

The partnership's technique of modelmaking comes originally from the ceramic industry, where moulds for new shapes have always been produced from models rather than technical drawings. Projects go directly from a model stage into mass production, and so modelmaking is still a skilled profession within the industry. Traditionally, the model is done by turning a lump of plaster of Paris either freehand or on a wheel or lathe, and this is still the way that Queensberry Hunt produce their models today. As Martin Hunt explains, it is much more exact a discipline than drawing: "You'd never find out a lot of things unless you made models. You do a little thumbnail sketch in your notebook and it seems to have something about it, so you try to reproduce that, but it's difficult to get the speed and fluidity that's in the drawing into the final product. That's the skill of it really, if you can do it." Relying so heavily on modelling in their work, Queensberry Hunt have improved

Left: The final technical specifications for Tournee reveal the complexity of an apparently simple design. Below: To produce the eventual design for Tournee, Martin Hunt modelled an entire series of prototypes for the handles. It is through this kind of detailed modelling that a design is refined

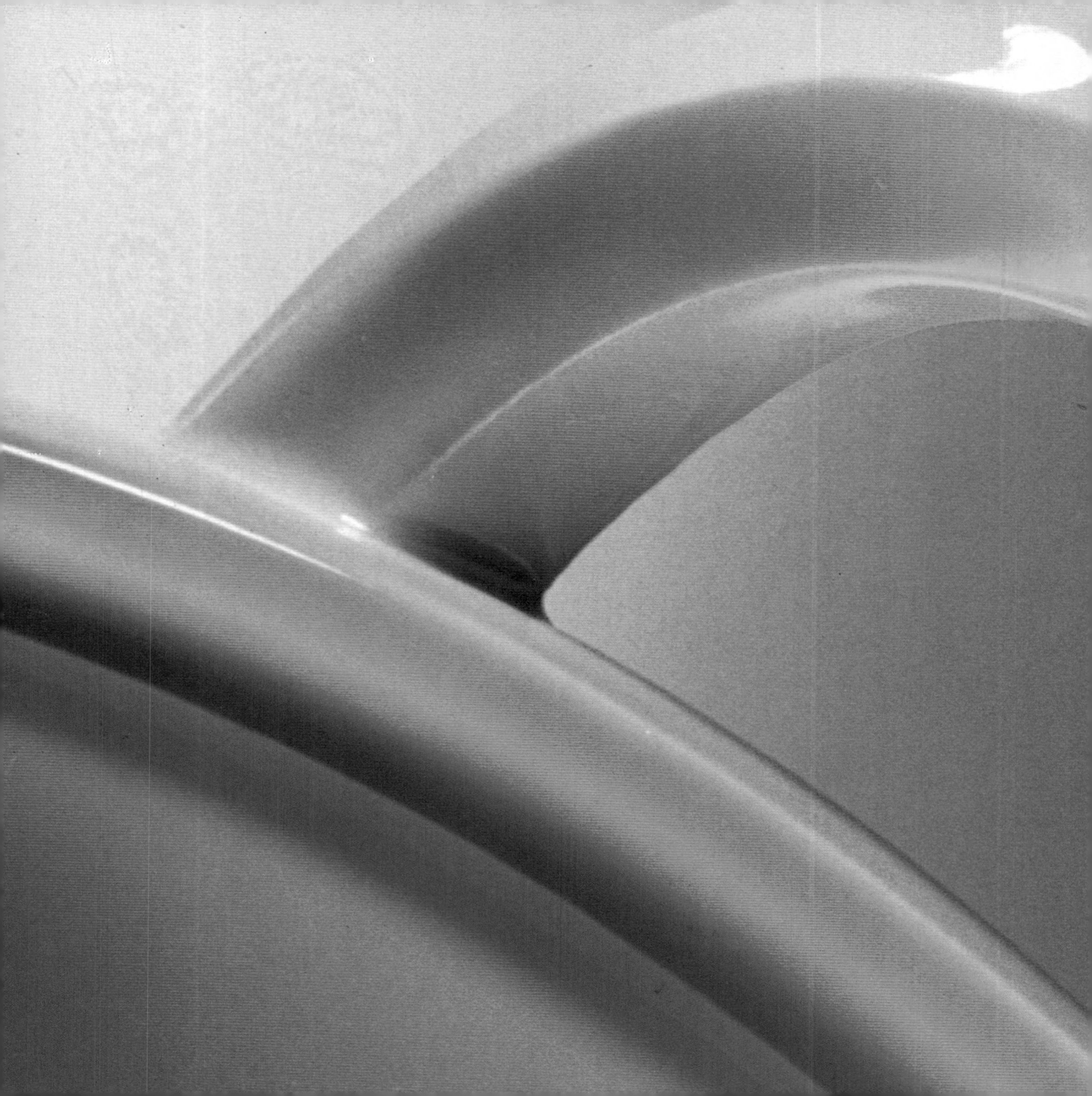

Left: Tournee's design combines a number of simple geometric shapes: the soft square, the oval and the pure circle. Right: In 1989 Rosenthal commissioned Martin Hunt to design one of a whole series of Artist's Cups. The model, shown here with the final product, reveals the sort of detail that plaster modelling makes possible

the process in order to suit their own techniques and situation. For example, plaster models are impregnated with resin to increase their strength, so that they can be sent to manufacturers, even abroad, quite safely. The design method has been speeded up by using insulating foam for what is called "sketch modelling", to rough out an idea before committing it to the far more detailed and time-consuming process of working in plaster. And even then, as Martin Hunt points out, "you have to expend energy many things that are going to be thrown away."

However, despite the fact that it is such a complex and time-consuming process, a Queensberry Hunt design can go through as many as nine or ten models before it is resolved. This is, again, an attitude which originated in their experience with ceramics, where the archetype of the product has already been established before any work begins. Says Hunt: "If you go into a china and glass department, teacups are dimensionally very similar anyway, and so our world has to be one of fine tuning. There just isn't the drastic change to the teacup which makes it quite different from any teacup which has gone before." This kind of effort can encompass every aspect of a design, from the depth and size of a plate to the precise placing of a knob or a handle on a cup.

It is an outlook which cannot simply be ascribed to the whim or the perfectionism of the designer; the partners also believe that these sorts of tiny details can contribute substantially to the success or failure of their work in the marketplace. Hunt continues: "In that sort of microsecond when the consumer picks up our cup and thinks, 'Shall I have it or not?', it is that bit of moving it from eight to nine that counts and fine tuning that gets you there." And while a detail of one or two millimetres difference may be insignificant visually, it can make all the difference to how a cup feels when it is held or when one drinks from it. These small refinements can be what persuades a buyer that they enjoy using a particular design, and want to replace breakages or add to their collection, thus turning a range into a steady seller over the years.

The work which they put into modelmaking and fine tuning is not considered by Queensberry Hunt to be an extravagance but rather an essential investment of time. Robin Levien believes that this approach is something that "changes the whole culture of how we work and what we do." In contrast to fee-earning designers who are just concerned with getting one job finished and moving on to the next one, the long-term success of a project is important to the partnership; because they work on a

The simple curves of Tournee are enhanced by the translucence of the fine porcelain

royalty basis, it benefits them directly. As a result, the amount of effort which they are prepared to put into getting something exactly right is not just a measure of their professional standards, it is also a shrewd investment.

However, this attention to detail is not just commercially motivated, since the realm of small differences is also important to visual design in tableware. The limitations imposed by Queensberry Hunt's desire to work in a modern idiom, and the fact that cups and plates are traditionally supposed to be certain shapes, means that the distinctiveness of the design has to be resolved in small details. In the design of Tournee, which has a very plain and contemporary feel to it, Martin Hunt used what he saw as a traditional design, "it is a soft oval egg form which is such a very conventional shape; maybe you do it a bit better or maybe it looks a bit cleaner, but it is still a basic pottery shape." The features which then transform the design into something very different are details such as the twisted handles butted directly against the cup and the softly squared-off shape of the plates. Henk Staal, Rosenthal's design director, explains why he thinks Tournee works, "It is different – but not too different. If a shape is too unadventurous or too distinctive it will fail. The handle-twist gives distinction to a very understandable shape."

It is getting that distinctive touch into the design which is important, and it is something at which Queensberry Hunt excel. Robin Levien cites Charles Eames, who said that he always liked to slip an ugly bit into his designs. The term "idiosyncratic" might be perhaps more appropriate, but the point is that a design has to have some character. Queensberry Hunt often refer to this kind of detail as a "trick" – the distinctive touch which livens up a design. They aim "to answer the brief and then put in a twist, some sculptural detail perhaps. The ultimate goal is a product with real personality that people can respond to." These details, such as the swan on Concept and the fine lines on Trend, form a hallmark of all their most successful designs, and indeed the initial idea for Tournee came from precisely this intention of creating a modern design "with a twist".

Queensberry Hunt do not see the modelmaking process as something which is only relevant in a traditional industry such as pottery. For them, the technique as embodies a particular attitude towards the finished object, an emphasis on both form and usability. Even in designs where the finished product would be made from technical drawings, as with the designs for cookware produced for Corning, the initial design was still developed from models. Only when they were satisfied with the form did they make the

Microfun, a cookware range which Martin Hunt designed for Thomas, is practical, designed to stack, and is easy to handle when hot. The inspiration for the handles is consciously Japanese

technical drawings, from the model. David Queensberry believes that too often the fact that industrial design is a form of sculpture is neglected: "The making of a complex three-dimensional object is a sculptural activity, but with the intention that the thing will have to perform a certain function and fit into a certain space. Nevertheless, it still remains a 3-D form that in our opinion cannot be totally resolved from a drawing." He feels that many objects which are produced solely from drawings and renderings lack a sense of form: "You can see why many industrial products are so awful; they are badly resolved because it's difficult to know what 3-D object a drawing describes." The concept of a sculptural form is also highly applicable to their work within tableware, as John Horler explains: "A cup is a very tactile object; if it invites you to pick it up, fondle and use it, then the designer has done a good job."

While such attention to form may have come from their backgrounds in ceramics, ironically it is something which is not best suited to the demands of an industry where nearly 80 per cent of tableware is sold decorated. Many Queensberry Hunt designs rely on sculptural details rather than pattern for their effects. The most obvious example of this is Trend, but a whole series of designs produced by all the partners – for example Martin Hunt's Concept range, John Horler's Astral design for Poole and the Bianca and Roulette ranges for Habitat – have relied on a surface texture. Says Queensberry: "We have not been particularly good at developing saleable surface decoration for the shapes we design. On the other hand, most of the people we work for haven't been very successful at developing it either." Throughout the industry, the development of pattern is a problem: a pottery firm may reject 100 patterns for every five that it accepts, and even then there is no guarantee that any of these will be really successful. David Queensberry also believes there is a significant problem even beyond this: their tastes in pattern, and those of most designers, simply do not mesh with those of the mass market. He thinks that: "the average designer prefers white or minimally decorated pottery, and there is a conflict between the requirements of the mass market and what you might term 'the tastes of the cognoscenti of design'."

While pattern is an important factor, Queensberry would also argue that without a good shape as a basis, no pattern will sell. "What is important is that you don't need shape that often. The requirement for pattern greatly exceeds that for shape, but a good pattern can never redeem a bad shape." This is not to say that Queensberry Hunt eschew pattern altogether in their work; they have

A number of products with traditional references have been designed by Queensberry Hunt for mass retailers, including the Provence pattern for Marks and Spencer (left), traditional "Oxford" tableware by T G Green (below) and modern salt-glaze stoneware by Moira, both for Habitat (bottom)

been involved in pattern development for a number of their shapes, and also came up with the "Provence" design for Marks and Spencer which, although originally developed for tableware, was extended into a whole range of kitchenware products.

One interesting way in which Queensberry Hunt have come to terms with pattern is by exploring more traditional forms of surface effect and decoration. Most patterned ceramics are decorated with printed transfers, but as David Queensberry points out, this is just one of the many techniques which have been used for ornament in the past. "Modern industrial methods have eliminated a whole world of qualities using ceramic materials and processes – today there is probably far less variety available to the consumer than there has been for hundreds of years. If you go to the V&A and look at the range of techniques and qualities that were available in the past, it is clear that modern industry has concentrated on certain techniques that could be mechanised and became very good at them." Queensberry Hunt's designs have explored the possibilities of using older methods of decoration for mass production, not only with *terra sigillata* for the Hornsea Concord shapes, but also in work for other, smaller firms. They developed a modern way of simulating the traditional technique of salt

Having failed to persuade Wedgwood to introduce marbled ceramics, David Queensberry eventually convinced Rosenthal to adopt the idea. This bowl is a double-cast pre-production prototype. Although this technique produced superior results, it proved to be too difficult for commercial production

glazing which eliminated the noxious fumes normally produced in the course of the original process. Their reworked version of salt-glazing, now suitable for mass production, was used to glaze old-fashioned casseroles which were sold in Habitat. They have also worked with TG Green, the manufacturer of the traditional blue-striped Cornish Kitchenware, to make other designs which would exploit their expertise in hand-turning.

The way in which Queensberry Hunt stress their own craft background and knowledge of the history of ceramics does not necessarily make them a group of technological Luddites, unthinkingly rejecting any form of new development or mechanisation in the industry. Although their work has shown a deep interest in past techniques and the history of ceramics, it forms just part of a wider knowledge of all aspects of production. This detailed understanding of the industry is something that is vital to their approach; they can, as in their work for Doulton Insulators and Henry Watson's, use a knowledge of manufacturing to see that products are made effectively. In addition, when dealing with larger factories as designers, they know whether or not it will be possible to put a design into mass production. While companies such as Rosenthal and Hornsea may be prepared to take all necessary steps to ensure that a design can be made as it has been designed, with many other companies, Queensberry Hunt have found it very useful indeed to know if, when a manufacturer says that an effect is not possible, whether this is actually the case or not.

The range of Queensberry Hunt's knowledge also extends to the new technology available to them, and they are equally prepared to use very modern methods as a means of producing new and different designs. This has been the case ever since Martin Hunt's work at Hornsea, where the technical innovations developed by Colin Rawson were an important part of the final designs. More recently, large pottery manufacturers have within the last decade begun to make plates by means of a new process known as dust-pressing. Plates are pressed out of a powdered clay rather than being "jollied", that is, produced on a spinning mould. The process is very efficient, and most manufacturers use it to churn out their existing designs more quickly. But Queensberry Hunt realised that, because the new machine pressed the plates out flat rather than spinning them, it removed some previous limitations since it was now possible to produce asymmetrical and non-circular plates. This idea was fed into the designs for Tournee, where the quartic plates could not have been

Left and opposite: Queensberry Hunt introduced computer-cutting, a technique originally developed for use on glass, to Wedgwood. These tests use the technique on jasperware to reveal fine layers of different colours beneath
Below: Isostatic dust pressing has made the production of new flatware shapes possible

made by the older jollying system. However, technology, and in particular production costs, can also place considerable limitations on a design such as Tournee. Here it was the square shape specified by Martin Hunt which proved too expensive for all the pieces: "We could have had soft-square salad bowls, but the casting process required would have been much more expensive – also, I am not unhappy with the restriction. It is good to have variety in a range, and I like the idea that some pieces would be square, some oval and some round."

Another technological development which occupied Queensberry Hunt for a number of years was the use of computerised cutting techniques. Their first contact with the process came during the course of some research work with a machine at the Royal College. The machine had originally been devised for the computer cutting of glass, but Queensberry Hunt realised that it could also be used to cut a hard ceramic material such as jasperware. Along with Wedgwood, Martin Hunt devised a number of designs for the material where cuts revealed different coloured layers of jasper underneath the top coat. The designs exploited the potential of the cutting machine, and produced cuts of a straightness and evenness that no human craftsman could ever have matched.

On the production line

Queensberry Hunt's designs for Thomas are manufactured from porcelain, valued as perhaps the finest of all ceramic materials because of its whiteness and translucence. Invented in China about 900 AD, porcelain was imported to the West beginning in the fifteenth century, although the technique of its manufacture was only discovered in Europe several hundred years later. Porcelain today is very similar to the original Chinese recipe, but the methods of production are now very different.

The basic porcelain paste is used in three forms: a plastic material like potter's clay, a liquid form known as "slip", and a dried dust. The plastic material is used for making cups, bowls and plates, in a process called "jollying", in which the paste is pressed against a rotating mould. For larger, hollow items such as teapots, jugs and gravy boats, liquid slip is poured into a porous plaster mould. The water in the slip is absorbed by the plaster and a deposit of porcelain is left on the mould; the length of the casting process determines the thickness of the article. High-pressure casting techniques have recently been introduced to the industry, and as a result, casting times have decreased from hours to minutes.

The most advanced technique for manufacturing ceramics is dust pressing, which is now the preferred technique of plate production at Thomas. The porcelain dust is injected into a mould and pressed isostatically, a system which results in very high production speeds and a more uniformly accurate product.

Before the made ware can be fired, minor blemishes and seam lines are removed with scrapers and sponges, in a process known as "fettling". It is then loaded on to kiln cars which are pushed through the tunnel kiln. The first, or biscuit, fire takes place at under 1000°C, a relatively low temperature which is simply to give the ware a reasonable strength so that it can be handled for glazing.

The glaze can be applied by either dipping or spraying. Although both of these processes can be automated, hand-dipping is very efficient and still used by the majority of factories. Some of the glaze is then removed from the foot of the pieces so that they don't stick to the surface when fired. (Because cups are inverted during the firing process, glaze is removed from the rim.) The glaze firing takes place at approximately 1400°C, to give the hardest glaze on any domestic ceramic. The glazed feet of the objects and the rim of the cups are polished, and if the porcelain is to be decorated, this is usually done by transfer. In a final operation, these are applied to the glazed surface and refired at a lower temperature, around 1200°C.

Previous page: Slugs of extruded plastic porcelain waiting to be processed. Right: Mould being placed in a bowl-making machine

Automated system of fettling plates after isostatic pressing. The system involves the movement of plates by vacuum pick-up

Previous page: High-pressure casting of a large rectangular dish. Slip, or liquid porcelain (clay particles in suspension) is injected under high pressure into a porous mould. This system has reduced casting time from hours to minutes. Right: A slip-cast coffee pot is removed from the plaster mould

A multiple plaster mould for the production of loop handles, used on the lids of coffee pots

Previous page: Clayware ready for the first (biscuit) firing in a tunnel kiln. The ware is fired as a line of cars is pushed through the length of the kiln. In the fast-fire cycle, entry-to-exit time is about 5 hours. Right: Bases of the oil and vinegar bottles awaiting assembly

Even in highly mechanised factories, there is still a considerable amount of skilled craft work. Here, the top sphere of the oil and vinegar bottle is being joined to the base

"Sticking up" – handles and cups are made separately, then joined with slip. Surplus slip is cleaned off in a subsequent process

Application of glaze by hand-dipping. This system, over a thousand years old, is still a very quick and efficient glazing method

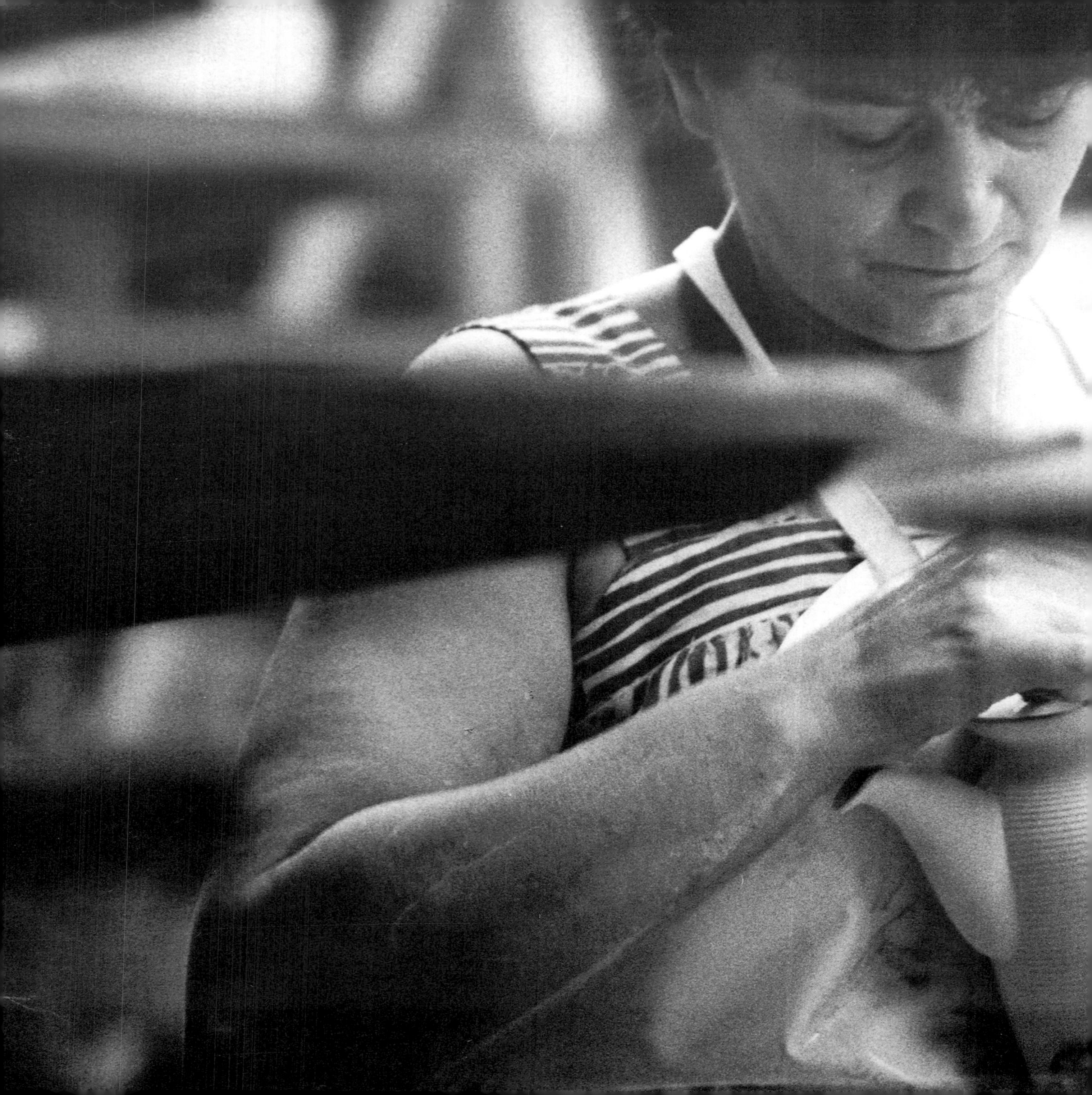

Previous page: Fettling of the top to ensure a precise and neat lid fit. Below: Inspecting, finishing and sponging the clayware before the biscuit firing

Final sponging of a coffee pot to remove the seams which are inevitable in a slip-casting system

Previous pages: Bowls ready for the final high-temperature glaze firing. The highest temperatures (1410°C+) occur in the centre of the kiln, which has a capacity of 12 tons of porcelain a day.
Below: Trend, the highest volume product designed by Queensberry Hunt, placed ready for the final phase

Right: Trend tableware before packing. More than 4 million pieces of Trend are made each year at the Thomas am Kulm factory in Germany

Chapter Six

Creativity and industry

One of Robin Levien's Domi range of taps for Ideal Standard

Thomas's Trend was so successful that it was expanded to include a number of different tabletop products, including stainless steel cutlery

In recent years Queensberry Hunt have been able to use some of the very particular working practices which they have developed on products other than just ceramics. Having made their reputation in one field, they have subsequently broadened the range of their designs. Although this diversification initially involved products in related areas, for example other table items such as woodware and cutlery, more recent design projects have also included bathrooms and telephones.

Expanding the range of design which they are prepared to undertake has not been a completely straightforward process in every case. To a certain degree, companies become typecast by the designs that they have already produced, and so after fifteen or more years in ceramics Queensberry Hunt did find it difficult to convince potential clients that they could handle projects in different materials.

When first commissioned to produce telephone prototypes for British Telecom, there were endless quips about pottery handsets. The consultancy also faced what amounted to a lack of credibility. Robin Levien feels that the design of ceramics is not perceived as part of the product design mainstream: "cups and saucers and dishes are not seen to be industrial design – they're something else," and so work outside this field has been harder to come by.

Queensberry Hunt's first work for Ideal Standard, Abstracts, was in the area of ceramic techniques, using reactive tranfers on suites and other co-ordinating items such as tiles (pattern design by Tricia Stainton)

As a result, the process of diversification has been slow and gradual. Opportunities have come from a number of different directions, and the initial successes were mainly an organic development which stemmed from the partnership's earlier activities in tableware and ceramics. The first impetus to diversify in fact followed from the success of Trend. Both Thomas and Queensberry Hunt realised that the immense popularity of the design provided an opportunity to develop a complete range of tabletop products which could be sold along with the original crockery and glass, and so matching ranges of both cutlery and wooden tableware were produced. The cutlery was a relatively simple derivative of the original design; fine ridges running down the handles echoed the decorative treatment of the porcelain, but such an effect could not be achieved on woodware. Here, the elliptical edge detail of the porcelain was greatly enlarged to become the distinctive feature of the design. The woodware in particular was a great success for Thomas, who had up until then had only sold glass and porcelain products, and Thomas have since gone on to sell other woodware ranges independently of their tableware designs.

A further opportunity for Queensberry Hunt to expand their range of product design came from their involvement with the bathroom manufacturers Ideal Standard, even though the company had first become interested in working with Queensberry Hunt precisely because of their ceramic background. It was a chance meeting between Martin Hunt and John Laughton, an Ideal Standard manager, resulted in Queensberry Hunt being asked to apply their experience of ceramics to explore different surface treatments for basins. A range of different experiments were undertaken, including inglaze reduction lustres and reactive transfers which produce a textured effect. The latter were actually put on the market, but were only moderately successful, although Ideal Standard believe that this was not a negative response to the designs themselves, but rather due to the fact that shape not pattern is by far the most important factor in selling their products.

It was this initial project, however, which led to Queensberry Hunt being commissioned for the design work which became Studio. The brief was to produce a bottom-of-the-range suite. As this would be largely determined by cost and production factors, the design initially had such a low priority that Ideal Standard felt that it barely justified the work of a designer. Roger Cooper of Ideal Standard remembers that he didn't think that

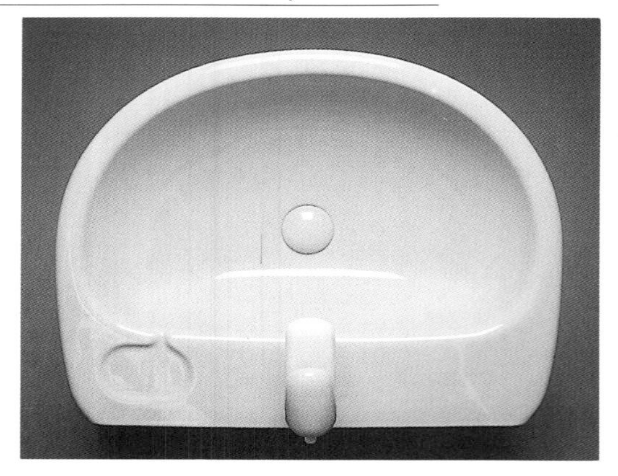

Left and below: The simple bowl shape of the Studio basin is perhaps the most distinctive feature of the whole range

Queensberry Hunt would be either interested or suitable: "I had this idea that Queensberry Hunt were going to be a design group that was only interested in the top end of the market and that a suite that was going to be very constrained by manufacturing and low production and unit costs would not appeal to them at all." Cooper believed that the partnership would prefer to work on new luxury lines, but Queensberry Hunt persisted until they became one of three design groups pitching for the job.

The brief mainly reflected the production orientation of the project – "giving a designer a three-inch wad of numbers doesn't get the creative juices flowing," comments Levien, "but underlying it all was the idea that producing it had to be as easy as shelling peas." Nonetheless, market research had also identified a desire for the more rounded styling which became the main feature of Studio. The arc of the bowl shape, as well as the distinctive soap dish, was therefore a feature of Queensberry Hunt's design from the start.

Moving into a new area of design was not to be a completely straightforward process however. After presenting Ideal Standard with a number of treatments, one was picked out for further development, and as Robin Levien remembers, Queensberry Hunt's previously tried

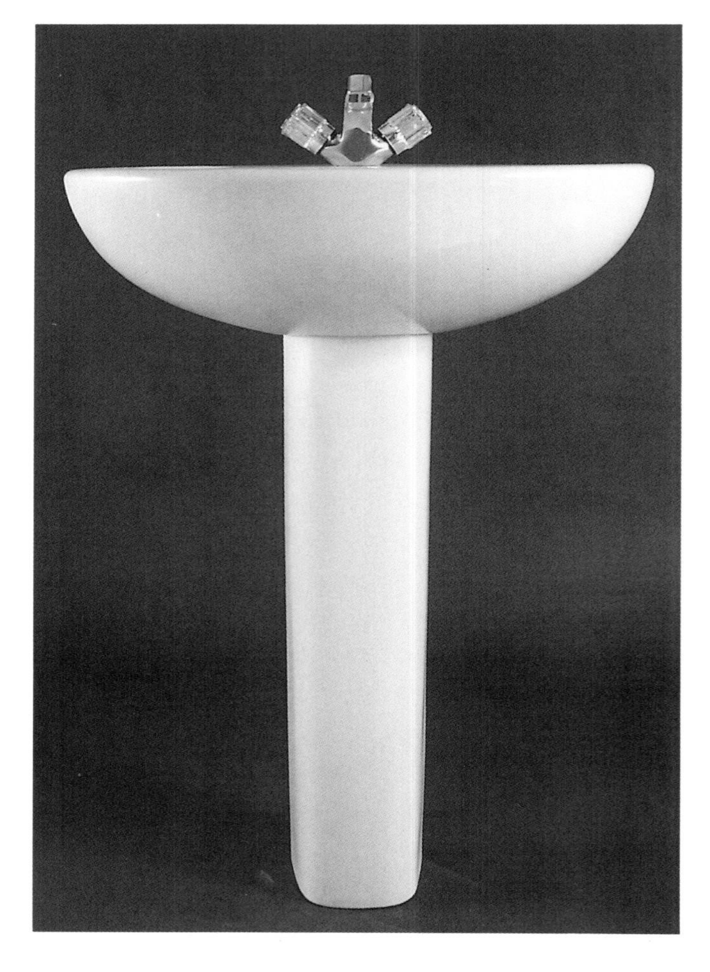

Queensberry Hunt's first "labour-intensive" plaster model for the Studio basin incorporated all the basic design features of the final suite

and tested working methods were not necessarily the most appropriate. They made a full-size model of their design in their usual material, plaster of Paris: "it was immaculate – it took three weeks to make and we even spent two days making a box to put it in." It was only when the partnership came to present their work that they discovered that two rival contenders for the commission had made their models in the rather simpler material of wood. Even though Levien believes that it was Queensberry Hunt's painstaking attention to detail which won them the job, he admits that if they had to do it all over again again, they would probably make a model in wood or fibreglass. Nowadays, though, Queensberry Hunt are more than accustomed to working in the field of sanitary ware and have evolved their own techniques for its design. This involves innumerable full-size models carefully pieced together from sections of blue foam – these permit the evaluation of not only the aesthetics, but also the ergonomics of the design.

One of the main things which Queensberry Hunt discovered in the course of developing Studio was the degree to which the production limitations were to determine the design. There are enormous difficulties in the manufacture of sanitary ware, many of which can affect the final design. For example, there are considerable technical problems involved in designing a shape which will not distort during firing. All products must also taper slightly to facilitate easy extraction from the mould, and because of the characteristics of the glaze used, all edges must have a substantial radius in order for the glaze not to break and leave a white line. At this stage of the project, Robin Levien felt that, as designer, his role also included that of guardian of the product's design identity within the production limitations. He found himself arguing that, for example, just because no one looks behind the base of a toilet, it doesn't mean that it can be left as a mass of snakelike pipework, and the resulting Studio closet adopted a clean, neat and slightly more expensive-looking base. Roger Cooper believes that negotiating with a designer in this way, although demanding, is ultimately rewarded by a better product: "Robin will argue about small details, but in the end I have to agree – he is almost always right."

The battles fought during the development of Studio were not all internal. One thing that Queensberry Hunt discovered when they began working in the field was that the squared-off shape common to the majority of cheap basins was not in fact the result of some obscure consumer preference, but was rather because of a British Standard which specified the size of the brackets on to

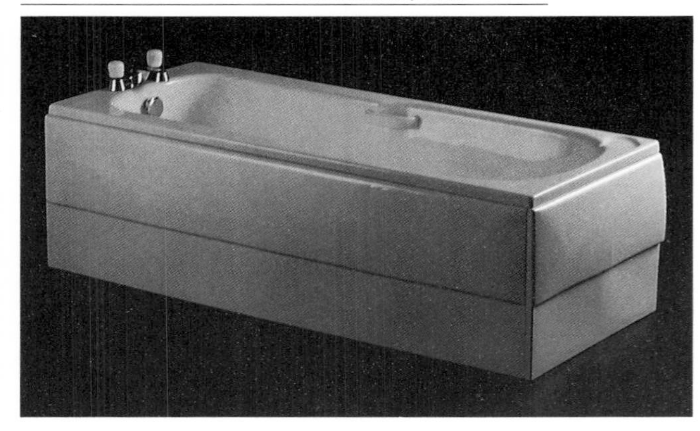

The grip on the Studio bath was developed especially for the range. It was formed by a revolutionary gas-filled moulding process which permits the use of colour-matched plastic instead of the traditional chrome

which such basins had to fit. Most manufacturers, rather than making more work for themselves, had stuck to this squarer basin as the only one in their ranges. Studio, on the other hand, therefore, has retained one rectangular British Standard basin, and then introduced a main range of round ones. In addition, the British Standard demands that taps be positioned 405mm apart, apparently in order to prevent users hitting their heads on them, something which can only serve as a testimony to the superior intelligence of mixer tap users.

It took a number of years to develop Studio from the initial brief, written in 1981, to its launch in 1986. During this period the product had metamorphosed from the original idea into a product which ultimately caught the imagination of the design press. As Robin Levien describes: "It went from being really a non-design project to being a design story and going straight on to the front cover of *Design* magazine when it was launched. The world had changed in the period between when it was conceived and when it came out. Roger ended up referring to it as a designer bathroom and he had started out by saying that it wasn't a design opportunity." Studio did undoubtedly become a design story. It was a runner up in awards for design effectiveness and won a prize in the first series of the BBC Design Awards – an uncharacteristically high-profile event for Queensberry Hunt.

Although bathroom design is very different from tableware, it is an area which is ideally suited to Queensberry Hunt's approach. The shape is the essence of sanitary ware design, indeed John Laughton who was at that time with Ideal Standard, echoes Queensberry Hunt's own approach when he refers to their products as "the sculpture business". Robin Levien would also argue that many of the design problems posed by its production are similar to those that the partnership had faced before: "It is still ceramics. You are still dealing with moulds with negative shapes, and unless you remember that, you can lose track very easily. Teapots and toilets are still made from the same difficult material – it can crack or distort in the firing, and the process is basically identical."

Despite the difference in terminology and objects, Studio is still very much part of a recognisable Queensberry Hunt design idiom. It's simplicity and conscious understyling reflects the partnership's own taste, but is also a response to the specific market for Studio. Much sanitary ware at this price is used for contract and public housing work, and is being used by people who often have no choice about what is being installed. Studio's lack of conspicuous styling

The Studio range was extensive enough to include a bidet, unusual at this level in the market

makes it easier to live with under these circumstances. For John Laughton, this is not simply a marketing strategy, although it has been very successful as such; it is also part of a very different attitude to design, almost a return to the ideals of "good design in everyday life".

Queensberry Hunt maintain that one of their fundamental tenets is the attitude that "there is no unresolvable conflict between good design and the mass market." Although it may seem almost old-fashioned in the light of recent perceptions of design as expensive surface styling, there is also a sense of the social responsibility of design. Terence Conran sees a similarity between Queensberry Hunt's approach and the ideals which led him to set up Habitat: "Like David, I have always been interested in the design of the ordinary. There are many designers who, whenever they design something, want to make a big statement with it. I think both of us would prefer to get a better pie dish or a better salad bowl into people's hands rather than the ultimate salad bowl." Conran attributes this attitude to the era in which both he and David Queensberry were starting out as designers: "Because we grew up in a particular time, the post-war reconstruction of Britain when everybody had a dream of improving the world, we don't think in quite the same kind of way that most contemporary designers would think. We were educated at that moment in British history when most designers thought – in a rather Bauhaus sort of way – that design had a strong social role to play."

The ideas of this period, that design should be interested in the design of everyday things, should involve good craftsmanship and above all be based in common sense, seem a very appropriate description of Queensberry Hunt's work. Their desire to bring good design to as many people as possible, as with Studio, does seem to link them more with the earliest consultancies such as DRU rather than with more recent generations of designers.

The design and thinking behind Studio made it a considerable success in the mass market sector for which it was intended; Levien calls it "a classic case of design being effective in the marketplace," and within a year it was forming 75 per cent of Ideal Standard's production. One reason for such impressive sales figures was that the arrival of Studio had brought the concept of design to a low-price sector where previously price alone had been the issue. Before the introduction of the Studio line, the bottom-end of every manufacturer's range had consisted of a mis-matched selection of products, united solely by virtue of being the same colour.

Computer-aided design was used extensively in the development of the Symphony range of bathtubs for American Standard, both in the initial options for the shapes and later for experimenting with colour combinations

In some ways the success of Studio presented Ideal Standard with a problem – the new range almost undermined their other products. The main difference between the most basic suite and an up-market one which could cost almost five times as much was design. The moment that design was introduced into the lower end of the product spectrum, there were fewer perceptible differences between the top and bottom ends of the range. Studio undoubtedly had some impact on the rest of Ideal Standard's ranges: it was obviously being bought by people who would otherwise have chosen a more expensive design, however, the company still feels that it made the right decision. The market was ready for a moderately priced, well-designed range and, had Ideal Standard not done so, one of their competitors would have certainly taken the opportunity to introduce it.

Again, one reason why Queensberry Hunt feel that their partnership with Ideal Standard has been so fruitful is because both companies share a common attitude to design, believing that good design is vital for the success of a range. Roger Cooper is convinced that the essential criteria for a successful product are "not just financial considerations – the product itself must also be something that all parties are happy to put their name to, something

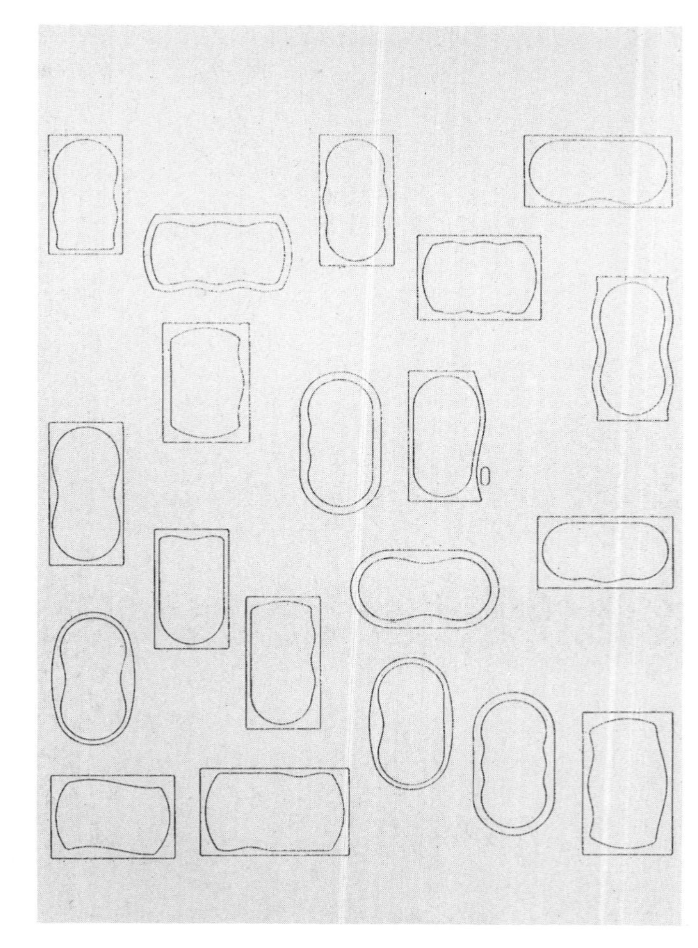

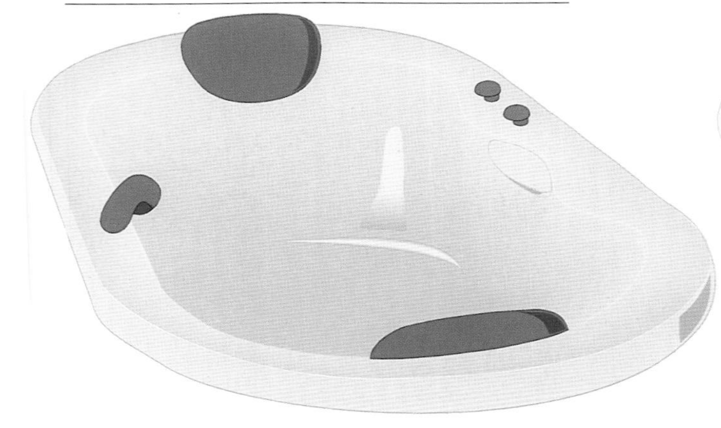

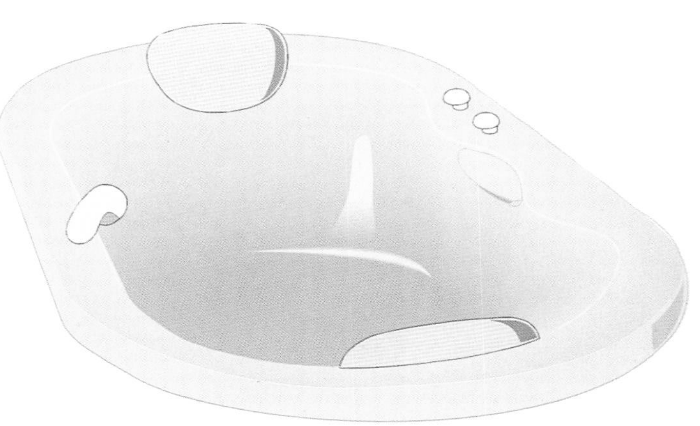

that Ideal Standard are proud to put on the market." Cooper also praises Queensberry Hunt's pragmatic attitude of seeking to design products that can be manufactured and will sell, rather than "isolating themselves in an ivory tower of design. They are prepared to accept the realities of life – they have always been prepared to look at problems and have a commercial approach."

The similarities between Ideal Standard's and Queensberry Hunt's philosophy are striking: both Roger Cooper and John Laughton echo the Queensberry Hunt view that the client bears considerable responsibility for the success of a design project, and argue that successful design management is a skill that many companies underestimate and fail to exercise properly. In the case of one of the handle styles for the Domi taps which Robin Levien designed for Ideal Standard, the ample amount of favourable press coverage which the design received ultimately failed to translate into the expected sales figures. Roger Cooper accepts, however, that the problem was not with the aesthetics of the product, but rather with the control that Ideal Standard exercised over the project: "We were just not rigid enough to say, 'No, that's not what we think the market wants.' All the designers might want them, but designers don't make up a major percentage of the UK buying public. We gave Robin a free range and perhaps we shouldn't have done."

Beyond these considerations, it is the personal relationship between designer and client which, although often neglected, is a crucial factor in the quality of the design produced. Roger Cooper feels that this has been an important part of Queensberry Hunt's, and in particular Robin Levien's, relationship with Ideal Standard. "Robin's personality suits Ideal Standard's personality, and he knows almost everyone in our organisation. It would be a difficult set-up to replace."

Queensberry Hunt's contacts with Ideal Standard did not end with the Studio suite and Robin Levien designed the Chloe range as well as a number of single baths for them in Britain. In addition, a considerable amount of work has also been done with Ideal Standard's sister company in the United States, following the move of their initial contact, John Laughton, to American Standard.

Queensberry Hunt's major work for American Standard has been on the Symphony range of whirlpool baths, launched in America in 1991. This became a major project for Queensberry Hunt and the production of so many large-scale objects stretched the resources of the consultancy almost to the limit. Although American Standard would

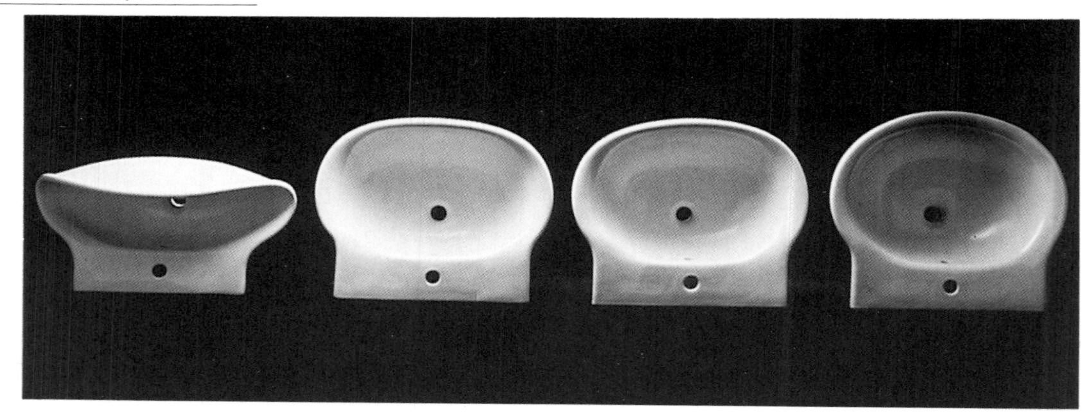

Prototype firings of the Chloe basin – technically very demanding to produce. A sanitary ware design may be refined many times before it emerges from firing in the intended shape

describe Robin Levien as the designer of the range, he himself stresses that the final designs were the result of creative teamwork between himself, Dave Tilbury, who works full-time for Queensberry Hunt and Dave Sherriff, who Levien drafts in for additional creative input on projects such as this.

Like many partnerships, Queensberry Hunt have always been faced with a dilemma when companies and magazines prefer to focus on the profile of an individual designer, when in fact the product was probably the result of a more team-based approach. Rather than promote the consultancy as a whole, the partnership has tended to credit the individual partner responsible for the project. This approach may, however, conceal the fact that most of their projects are the result of regular discussions and input from all the partners, as David Queensberry explains: "We've tended to work for separate clients, but we do depend on group criticism. We like to check with each other; it is important to have interaction between the partners." He feels that this mode of operation is necessary because of their decision to design products on a royalty basis. "Our way of working forces us to be hypercritical. If I think we are doing something wrong then I ought to speak up. We all listen to each other on that level, because the future of our business will depend on whether we were right or wrong. In the end, though, each design has to be the responsibility of one partner who must decide what goes ahead and what is presented to the client, since design cannot ultimately be decided by committee. We try to combine the advantages of individual people creating their own products with the advantages of interaction, criticism and teamwork. There are certain things like the complex relationship between the body, the spout, the handle, and the knob of the Tournee coffee pot that simply cannot be resolved by people sitting around and talking about it."

The development of the Symphony bath range marked a considerable departure from Queensberry Hunt's usual working methods in that Computer Aided Design (CAD) was used, in particular for the initial concept. The baths are all based on differing combinations of three geometric elements: curves, sine waves and lines. Rather than repeatedly drawing and redrawing such a complex piece of geometry as a sine curve, the computer was used to generate a large number of variations on the basic themes, and slight alterations could be made without starting from scratch. American Standard was presented with thirty different options for the range from which nine were selected for further development. Queensberry Hunt are

Below: the delicate rim on the Chloe basin, inspired by classic Chinese bowls. Right: foam sketch models for the Domi range of taps. The aim of Robin Levien's designs for Ideal Standard was that they should co-ordinate with the soft shapes of the rest of the bathroom fixtures

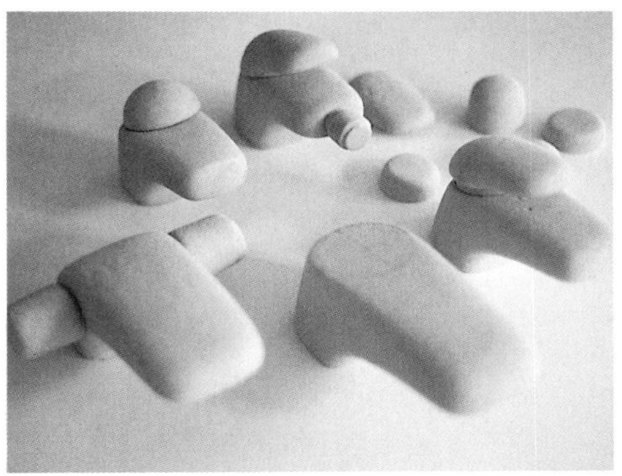

sure that the computer made it possible for them to make a more sophisticated presentation than would have otherwise been possible on a limited budget.

However, this interest in new technology does not imply a rejection of all their previous methods of work; once the nine shapes had all been agreed on, each was modelled and altered, often several times, in order to resolve problems such as handgrips or how the curves would be handled once they met the bottom of the bath. But, as Levien relates, very often the designs seemed to work themselves out: "We'd found a terrific theme into which everything was falling quite naturally." The rim of one of the tubs, for example, is narrow at the point of access and broad where the taps are. This sense of everything evolving quite logically once the basic decisions have been made was shared by Martin Hunt in designing Concept. Once it had been decided that concentric rings would be the main feature of the design, placing them on each different piece seemed to be suggested quite naturally by the various production methods, an experience which Hunt finds satisfying: "I think it's an indication that an idea's good if you don't hit problems like that on the technical side."

The Symphony range of baths has received an enthusiastic response as well as several awards after its

Previous page: one of Tricia Stainton's experimental pattern designs for Queensberry Hunt. Right: After initial experimentation on CAD, each of the American Standard Symphony shapes was modelled at one-sixth scale to resolve the details of the shape

launch in America. This may seem slightly surprising since, to European sensibilities, the biomorphic design and somewhat post-modern colours seem remarkable, almost overdone for a bathroom. However, in America, this kind of bath is not so much a utility product meant to satisfy the functional requirements of getting clean as a leisure activity in itself. Queensberry Hunt's design recognises this, and although the Symphony range may differ considerably from traditional bathroom products, it is not in fact as light-hearted as it might at first appear.

Both the American Standard range and Martin Hunt's most recent York range for Thomas show the influence of the times, with post-modernist aspects of style and colour as well as more distinctive designs which differ greatly from the comfortable understyling of Trend. Hunt explains that, "if post-modernism is an influence, then it is something which is all over with. Charles Jencks would yawn, 'that was years ago!' What we are doing is interpreting things and feeding them in, but it is actually behind the times in terms of designer fashion trends." Queensberry Hunt's commercial goals do place certain restrictions on the degree to which they can be part of the vanguard of design, but this is something that they recognise and accept as the consequence of their other objectives.

Gradually moving into the field of bathroom products has been part of an organic process for Queensberry Hunt. Although it began as an involvement with the technical, ceramic side, their work for Ideal Standard and American Standard has now gone far beyond this. The baths are all acrylic, a material which presents very different problems for the designer, and they are now also producing designs for taps. As a result, they have been led fully and almost unwittingly into the world of "real" industrial design and products which require engineering drawings.

In a rather oblique fashion, the Studio design also provided Queensberry Hunt with further inroads into this world through the BBC Design Awards. British Telecom, as sponsors, gave their own award which went to Studio. The prize was a design commission for BT, and an opportunity to present ideas for the next generation of mobile handsets which has since become quite a successful area for them. The BT brief was for a "blue skies" pocket telephone, but the project received a considerable amount of publicity and ultimately led to more work in the field, first for STC and then for Mercury. These projects have received a certain amount of television coverage, and were exhibited in the Design Museum for quite some time, but Queensberry Hunt's commercial instincts are not satisfied with this:

Right and below: The wave line chosen for the shape of the Rondo bath in the Symphony range allows for accessories such as this filler to be integrated into the form of the bath

As a highly skilled engineer and modelmaker, Dave Tilbury has contributed greatly to many of the partnership's designs

Below: This concept model for the personal pocket phone was developed for British Telecom Mobile Communications by Robin Levien and Dave Sherriff. Opposite: Among later commissions in this field was this concept model of a PCN handset for Mercury Personal Communications, designed by Robin Levien in conjunction with Chris Murray

"We've got models in showcases and we've been featured in magazines, but the proof of the pudding is in having things for sale out there in the stores and we haven't got there yet." Queensberry Hunt would like to develop this aspect of their work further, but Robin Levien admits to a certain disappointment that, so far, these designs have not been able to overcome the image of Queensberry Hunt as designers who only know about tableware: "I still believe that it makes sense for us to keep on trying, but it is amazing how blinkered people are when you show them what you have done in the past and try to convince them that you can do something else. For example, to get some work designing a camera, it's almost as if you'd already had to have done one – *and* it's got to be more than just a model of one."

Expanding into other areas of product design does not of course mean that Queensberry Hunt have abandoned ceramic design altogether. They have continued to work with Thomas on new ranges of tableware, and recent work for companies like Corning have included kitchenware products such as casseroles and microwave ware (Pyroflam cookware has been particularly successful). However, the number of European firms where this sort of design work is possible has become increasingly limited,

SERVICE
DIRECTORY
MESSAGES
CALL DIVERT
BATTERY
Call
Service
End
Select
1
2
3
4
5
6
7
8
9
*
0
#

John Horler's Shape 10 for Royal Porcelain in Thailand is one of the designs which has resulted from Queensberry Hunt's active approach to seeking design work abroad

and so the partnership has had to look to new markets. In recent years they have been working with a manufacturer in Thailand who hopes to emerge as a major supplier to the US tableware market. Their designs, although still plain and understated, have responded to this particular market and are more traditional in style than much of their previous work. "It is design that has moved slightly more in the direction of the classical – something like Shape 10 would look perfectly respectable with Laura Ashley."

Queensberry Hunt foresee an increasing portion of their business coming from the entrepreneurial aspect of the consultancy. An obvious example would be their design and development of a woodware collection manufactured in Thailand, an undertaking which followed from their previous tableware contacts. All the partners see these sorts of projects as important for expanding the range of design work open to Queensberry Hunt over the next few years. David Queensberry emphasises this point: "I think that the woodware project with Thailand may be typical of one aspect of our future development – you have an idea about being able to design and make something that there is a market for. You see an opening in the market – that's the vital thing. In these entrepreneurial ventures, it's no good designing something if you don't see an opening. You then set about finding the manufacturers, finding someone who understands the distribution side of things and create a joint venture."

In the course of working with firms in the Far East, the partnership came to realise that they could produce items in wood there at a price that it would be impossible to match in Britain. In the past one could obtain well-made wooden bowls manufactured in traditional centres such as High Wycombe, but today the price of both wood and its working in Britain have made such products prohibitively expensive, and these sorts of artefacts are now almost exclusively the preserve of the artist/craftsmen.

Queensberry Hunt recognised that this opportunity of working with the Thai companies would make the manufacture of well-designed wood objects at a reasonable price feasible. It was a way to fill a gap in the market with something desirable which would not have otherwise existed. For David Queensberry this kind of project gives a clear indication of how, in the future, Queensberry Hunt should not only be content to survive by working with existing clients such as Ideal Standard and Thomas, but should also continue to expand and diversify their range of experience, above all, making their own design opportunities.

Right, below and overleaf: Martin Hunt's most recent design for Thomas, York, which again represents a more formal approach to tableware

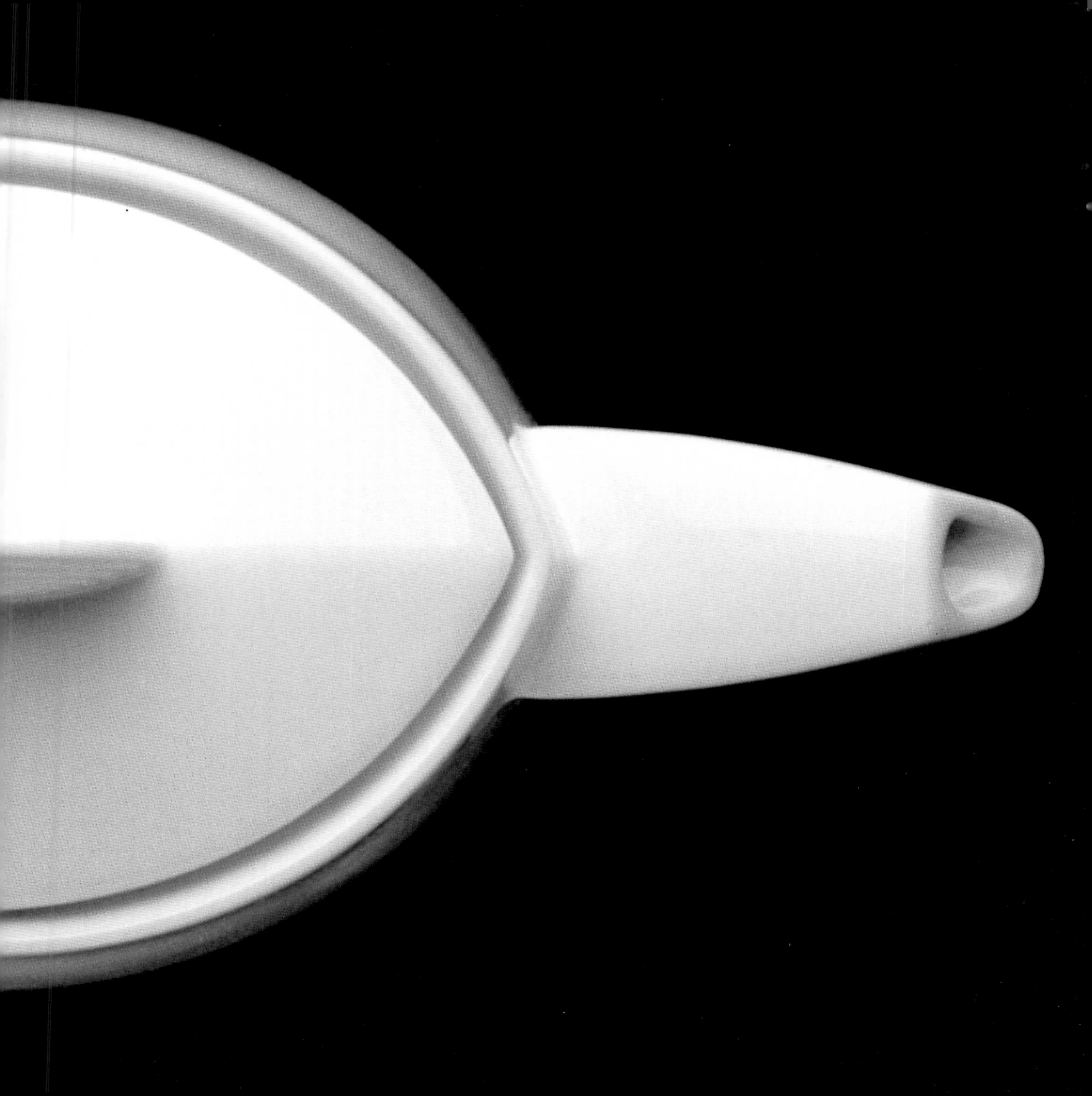

List of projects

Major Projects

1956
Queensbury Tableware
Manufacturer: Crown Staffordshire China
Designer: David Queensberry
(Also, a number of other products including tableware with patterns by various designers, candlesticks and a child's breakfast set (graphics by Bernard Blatch) which won an award in the first Design Council Awards in 1960)

1963
Webb Corbett cut crystal
Manufacturer: Webb Corbett
Designer: David Queensberry

Midwinter Fine tableware
Manufacturer: W R Midwinter
Designer: David Queensberry

1966
Midwinter Trend tableware
Manufacturer: W R Midwinter
Designer: David Queensberry

1967
Midwinter MQ2 tableware
Manufacturer: W R Midwinter
Designer: David Queensberry

1968
Pressed electrical porcelain giftware
Manufacturer: Wade, for JRM Designs
Designer: Martin Hunt

1970
Hexagonal ashtrays and vases
Manufacturer: Henry Watson's Pottery, for Habitat
Designer: Martin Hunt

Atlantis tableware
Manufacturer: Rosenthal/Celtic Ceramics, Eire
Designer: Martin Hunt

1971
Ceramic lamps
Manufacturer: Henry Watson's Pottery
Designer: Martin Hunt and James Kirkwood

1973
Delfi tableware
Manufacturer: Bing & Grøndahl, Copenhagen
Designer: Martin Hunt

Paolozzi Plates
Manufacturer: Wedgwood
Designer: Eduardo Paolozzi – Queensberry Hunt project

Shape 44 tableware
Manufacturer: Bing & Grøndhal, Copenhagen
Designer: Martin Hunt

Tea for One/Nesting Bowls
Manufacturer: Bing & Grøndahl
Designer: Martin Hunt

1974
Contrast tableware
Manufacturer: Hornsea Pottery
Designer: Martin Hunt

Coppa glassware
Manufacturer: Thomas
Designer: Martin Hunt

1976
Concept tableware
Manufacturer: Hornsea Pottery
Designer: Martin Hunt

1979
Bianca tableware
Manufacturer: Josiah Wedgwood and Co.
Designer: Robin Levien

1980
Concord tableware
Manufacturer:
Hornsea Pottery
Designer: Martin Hunt

1982
Original Suffolk
terracotta kitchenware
Manufacturer:
Henry Watson's Pottery
Designer: John Horler and
David Queensberry

1983
Trend tableware
Manufacturer: Thomas
Designer: Robin Levien

Trend glassware
Manufacturer: Thomas
Designer: Robin Levien

Flair tableware
Manufacturer:
Poole Pottery
Designer: John Horler

1984
Lyndhurst tableware
Manufacturer: Wedgwood
Designer: Martin Hunt

Sandie tableware
Manufacturer: Creative
tableware (Wedgwood
Group), for Habitat
Designer: Robin Levien
Oxford tableware
Manufacturer: T G Green,
for Habitat
Designer:
Queensberry Hunt

1986
Studio bathroom range
Manufacturer:
Ideal Standard
Designer: Robin Levien

Trend woodware
Manufacturer: Acme
Industries, Thailand,
for Thomas
Designer: Robin Levien

1987
Microwave cookware
Manufacturer:
Fraser & Glass
Designer: John Horler

Rosenthal Artist's Cup
Manufacturer: Rosenthal
Designer:Martin Hunt

Roulette tableware
Manufacturer:
Johnson Brothers
Designer: Martin Hunt
Trend cutlery
Manufacturer: Thomas
Designer:
Queensberry Hunt

1988
Provence tableware
Manufacturer: T G Green,
for Marks & Spencer
Designer:
Queensberry Hunt
and Vanessa Byrne

Astral tableware
Manufacturer:
Poole Pottery
Designer: John Horler

Domi taps
Manufacturer:
Ideal Standard
Designer: Robin Levien

1989
Chloe bathroom range
Manufacturer:
Ideal Standard
Designer: Robin Levien

Tournee tableware
Manufacturer: Thomas
Designer: Martin Hunt

1990
Cheltenham porcelain
Cookware
Manufacturer:
Siam Fine China
Designer: John Horler

Cheltenham woodware
Manufacturer:
Surina Thailand
Designer: Martin Hunt
and John Horler

Microfun cookware
Manufacturer: Thomas
Designer: Martin Hunt

Shape 10 tableware
Manufacturer:
Royal Porcelain
Designer: John Horler

Symphony bathtubs
Manufacturer:
American Standard
Designer: Robin Levien

1991
Shape 20 tableware
Manufacturer:
Royal Porcelain
Designer: John Horler

York tableware
Manufacturer: Thomas
Designer: Martin Hunt

Other projects

1975
Table lamps
Manufacturer: Doulton
Insulators, for Habitat
Designer: Martin Hunt
and Robin Levien

1976
Turned candlesticks
Manufacturer: Wade,
for Habitat
Designer:
Queensberry Hunt

1979
Ashtrays
Manufacturer:
A G Hackney, for Habitat
Designer: Robin Levien

Vases and cachepots
Manufacturer:
T G Green, for Habitat
Designer: Robin Levien

1983
Calypso vases
Manufacturer:
Poole Pottery
Designer: John Horler

1985
Ziggurat giftware
Manufacturer: A G
Hackney for Habitat
Designer: Robin Levien

1986
Granite vases
Manufacturer: T G Green
Designer:
David Queensberry
and Dave Tilbury

Nova bathroom
accessories
Manufacturer:
Hornsea Pottery
Designer: Robin Levien